THIS IMMORTAL PEOPLE

THIS
IMMORTAL
PEOPLE

A Short History
of the Jewish People

EMIL BERNHARD COHN

Translation from the German,
Prologue and Epilogue
by Hayim Goren Perelmuter

PAULIST PRESS
New York/Mahwah

for
Debbie, Mayer and Michael,
three beloved links in
the chain of this
immortal people

Library of Congress
Catalog Card Number: 84-62563

ISBN: 0-8091-2693-1

ᴏᴀʟᴄ: 12234457

Published by Paulist Press
997 Macarthur Boulevard
Mahwah, New Jersey 07430

Printed and bound in the
United States of America

Contents

Emil Bernhard Cohn

Emil Bernhard Cohn, a distinguished rabbi, writer and active Zionist in pre-Hitler Germany, was born in Berlin in 1881, the son of a co-worker with Theodore Herzl. He received his Jewish education at home. As a student he organized Zionist groups with J.L. Magnes, who later became the first President of the Hebrew University.

He was appointed Preacher (Prediger) for the Jewish Community of Berlin in 1906 and was forced to resign in 1907 because of his Zionist views. This event was the focal point of much polemic. He then served as Rabbi in Kiel and Essen, returning to Berlin in 1925.

He published plays under the pseudonym of Emil Bernhard, one of which, *Brief des Uriah* (Uriah's Letter), appeared in 1919 and was performed by the Habimah Theatre. He is principally remembered as the biographer of David Wolfsohn, successor to Theodore Herzl in the leadership of the Zionist movement. When Hitler came to power he was editor of a planned series of short books designed to give German Jews an insight into their identity with which many had been suddenly confronted. *Die Juedische Geschichte* (1936) was the only book of the series to appear in Germany, and it appeared in translation as *This Immortal People* (1945).

He reached the United States in 1939, just before the outbreak of World War II and resided in New York City until his death in 1948.

Hayim Goren Perelmuter

Hayim Goren Perelmuter, a native of Montreal, was ordained Rabbi at the Jewish Institute of Religion in New York, studied at McGill, Harvard and Hebrew Universities, and received his Doctorate from the Hebrew Union College-Jewish Institute of Religion in Cincinnati. He is Professor of Jewish Studies at the Catholic Theological Union in Chicago, Visiting Professor at the Pacific Lutheran Theological Seminary and Graduate Theological Union in Berkeley, and Rabbi Emeritus of the KAM-Isaiah Israel Congregation in Chicago. He is translator and interpreter of the works of David Darshan of Cracow, a contributor to the Theologische Realenzyklopaedie and translator from Yiddish, German and Hebrew.

Foreword

This little book has had a curious and remarkable history. It appeared in Germany in 1936, the first in a projected series of similarly brief volumes on Jewish culture and history. It turned out to be the only book in the series to be published, since the author, my late father, an outspoken Zionist activist and rabbi, had to flee the Nazis overnight in October of that year. While the series was meant to be of general Jewish interest it was primarily directed at those German Jews who, over the decades, had lost contact with their tradition and background and who now, under the increasing pressure of Nazi persecution, felt a sudden and deep need to be in touch with their origins again. It must be remembered that in 1936 most German Jews—and many non-Jews—still felt that Hitler was an aberration that would soon disappear. It turned out to be a false hope with tragic consequences. Still, at the time no reasonably thinking person, Jewish or not, could foresee the Holocaust.

In 1938, after a few years in Holland, Emil Cohn immigrated to New York. Among his books that were eventually published in English translation was this little Jewish history now titled *This Immortal People* (Behrman Jewish Book House, N.Y., 1945). The translation

1

was done in clear, lucid and excellent style by a young rabbi, H. Goren Perelmuter. The first edition was sold out and not reprinted.

It is to Rabbi Perelmuter's great credit that Paulist Press has now undertaken the publication of a revised and extended version of the book. Since the original work was completed before the Second World War, the Holocaust, and the rebirth of the Jewish spirit through the establishment of the State of Israel, additional material, covering these and other more current historical events, had to be added. Rabbi Perelmuter undertook this task with a great scholarly skill, insight and enthusiasm. In fact, it was Rabbi Perelmuter's enthusiasm for the book which kept it alive in the first place. During many years of teaching Jewish studies at Christian theological seminaries where he taught, Rabbi Perelmuter reproduced and utilized his translation of Emil Cohn's little history and found it to be an excellent text for his students. This experience led him finally to submit the book to Paulist Press which, happily, agreed to its republication. And so it came about that a book about Jewish history first written for the benefit of besieged German Jews thirsting for knowledge of their past now reappears, almost fifty years later, as one to teach Christian students the story of the Jewish people. It is hoped, of course, that it will be read by many more interested people, Jewish and non-Jewish alike.

I am deeply grateful to Rabbi Perelmuter for his continued interest in my father's little book which he nurtured through the years, and to Paulist Press which is now seeing to its revival in this expanded form. Above all, I am delighted that in this way my father's book will again be of benefit to students and readers who wish to know more about "This Immortal People" and their history.

Rabbi Bernhard N. Cohn
New York City

Prologue

In this instance, the old cliché "You can't go home again" does not hold. Sometimes you can.

Back in 1938 when my beloved teacher and mentor Stephen S. Wise introduced me to Emil Bernhard Cohn, recently arrived in New York as a refugee from Hitler Germany, and asked me to translate his little book on Jewish history, I was a senior at the Jewish Institute of Religion.

The author had imaginative goals for the book. He thought that it might ultimately be brought out as a little pocket paperback, perhaps by the Jewish Welfare Board to be issued to Jewish army personnel along with a pocket Bible and Prayer Book. It never turned out that way. *This Immortal People* came out instead as a hardcover book in 1945, sold out one edition and then went out of print.

For me the task began as a hack translating job to provide a struggling student in the latter years of the Great Depression with a little extra income. But as I worked on it, its succinct magic worked on me, and I was gripped by the compressed sweep—Jewish mystics call it *tsimtsum*—of his narrative. It was for me a thumbnail sketch par excellence, whose meaning pointed out not so much to the thumb, as to the "finger of God" in the history and destiny of four millennia of the historical experience of an immortal and imperishable people.

The translation was completed in late 1938. The translator was ordained the following year, deeply moved by the book he had translated, and by its conclusion heavily weighted with a combination of foreboding and hope, but not a glimmering of suspicion of what lay ahead—not the Holocaust, not Nagasaki and Hiroshima and the birth of the nuclear age, not the birth of the State of Israel and the return of the Jewish people to the company of nations.

Even the translator virtually forgot it. It rested on a shelf in his library. He thought of it occasionally with an affection tinged with nostalgia. But basically it was a product of his "salad days" and there were other things ahead to be done. Among these were congregational ministries in Waltham (Mass.), Johnstown (Pa.) and Chicago; and a second career in academics, at the Catholic Theological Union and the Chicago Cluster of Theological Schools and at the Pacific Lutheran Theological Seminary and Graduate Theological Union in Berkeley.

In the process of teaching a course on Current Issues in the Christian-Jewish Dialogue with Franklin Sherman, Dean of the Lutheran School of Theology at Chicago, the latter was looking for an appropriate short history of the Jewish people which could be read through in a few hours. He had tried several and they were not what he wanted. At that point I thought of *This Immortal People*, out of print and out of date though it be. That, he said, was just what he was looking for.

The enthusiastic student reaction to that short book, which they read, perforce in xerox form because copies were not available, persuaded me of the value of its republication, briefly updated, of course in the tenor of the book, to cover the momentous half-century of Jewish history that had ensued, a half-century that had four millennia of experience compressed in it as Emil Bernhard Cohn had himself compressed Jewish history. Perhaps you could go home again.

As has already been observed, the German version was published in 1936, and the English translation completed by 1939. The author added one paragraph, the second paragraph from the end of Chapter 26 of the translation, and it reads:

> This much is certain: this war which has engulfed the world in a terrible outburst of violence, as these lines are written, is neither an imperialistic struggle nor a fight to the finish between Capitalism and Socialism. So far as Adolph Hitler is concerned, it matters not whether one empire falls and another rises over its ruins, nor whether a new social order emerges. For him this is primarily a war against Judah and nothing more. This may sound like an arrogant claim from the pen of a Jewish historian. And yet it is profoundly true, and is further testimony to the eternal survival of Israel, the great mystery of world history. . . . Adolph Hitler has never contradicted himself, and ever proclaims it as his firmest and most inward conviction—that the Jew must be destroyed. And not only when he burns synagogues and murders Jews, but even when he persecutes the Church and imprisons priests—it is the eternal Jew that he has in mind. . . . And in his eyes, the Christian is nothing more or less than a Jew in disguise.

This added paragraph reflects a basic change in attitude to the Christian role in Jewish history that is to be found

in the rest of this brief volume of his. Its brief refer-
ences to Christianity are influenced by Cohn's percep-
tions of the somber relationships of the early centuries
and the Middle Ages, and of course the rise of the Nazis
to power. Nor had the author reason to detect any substantial change in the Christian attitude of the 1930's.
The silences, with just a few exceptions, were deafen-
ing, from the Vatican and from mainline Protestant
leadership.

What was not, indeed could not have been, reflected
in what he wrote when he wrote it were the changes in
Christendom itself, wrought by the Holocaust and the
birth of the nuclear age, that expressed itself in self-
searching, and in new dimensions of the Christian-Jewish dialogue, witness Vatican II and the thinking sensi-
tized by these events of a vast range of Protestant and
Catholic theologians, culminating, it seems to me, with
the insights of a Heiko Oberman, Jurgen Moltmann,
Friedrich Heer, Rosemary Ruether, and Clemens
Thoma, just to mention a few. The added paragraph to
which I have referred written shortly before his death
was a hint of Cohn's awareness of these new possibilities, many of which he never lived to experience.

The shocking impact of the Holocaust, with its six
million Jewish dead, and the almost simultaneous birth
of the State of Israel, were two events beyond the ken of
his study, and these missing components, together with
their consequences, will need to be dealt with. The
implications of the emergence of a Jewish State in a
world of nation states, now increased in number to well
over a hundred and twenty-five, is a new reality against
which some of Cohn's theories will need to be tested.

There is another significant omission, or, perhaps,
more precisely put, misinterpretation. This has to do

with the role of Jewish mysticism in Jewish history. Cohn is an heir to the rationalist tradition in Jewish history, with, one must add, Zionist-romantic overtones that almost border on mysticism. Yet he dismissed Jewish mysticism even more abruptly than he dismisses Christianity. The consequences of the magnificent work of Gershom Scholem in this field, and the explosion of research in this area by his followers, will need to be dealt with.

So, for that matter, will we need to consider the development of the American Jewish community as a diaspora Golden Age to match Spain, Poland and Babylonia. And we will need to take a look at the rebirth of Western Jewish communities and the stirrings of Soviet Jewry.

To fill these lacunae, and, hopefully, with the same kind of compactness, is the task of the epilogue which will follow Cohn's text. This will follow Chapter 26. I believe it is appropriate to reserve his own final chapter, the brief "Retrospect and Finale," so that this updated work can appropriately conclude with the author's own words.

For after all is said and done, despite the omissions, and despite some views we may not find as congenial as we might like, there is something in the sweep of his vision and the breadth of his view which touches the very substance of reality in history and provides a special kind of evidence of the reality of the Covenant in Jewish history.

And after half a century the book wears well. You can go home again.

Preface

The author of this little volume is well aware of the enormous difficulties involved in attempting to condense the more than forty centuries of Jewish history into the narrow space of one hour's reading. He has dared to make the attempt only because of his conviction that history is neither a sum nor a system of dates and events, but rather the stream and unfolding of vitally living forces. He has done so in the full consciousness that it is the duty of the historian to present in clear outline the inner forces behind the stream of a people's history, so that the people be made aware not merely of the chain of experiences in time and space, but also of the bright guiding star of its ideals and aspirations. It is left for the reader himself to judge how far he has succeeded in this attempt to etch as briefly but as graphically as possible a portrait of the Jewish people and its history down the corridor of the centuries and in the parade of the nations.

Emil Bernhard Cohn

1

This Was the Land

Canaan, homeland of the Jews, lies where the Syrian coastland touches the eastern edge of the Mediterranean and forms a fertile offshoot of that vast desert belt that stretches from Asia to Africa. Barren hills and valleys interspersed here and there with thirsty oases and meadows stamp the landscape to this very day with a stony mien. The winter rains that come in torrents overnight transform the parched river beds into madly coursing streams and give the earth a fruitfulness that in Biblical days earned for it the picturesque tribute marking it as "a land flowing with milk and honey." But often too, these rain-enriched streams are devoured by an inexorable sun and, when the heavens are "brassy and sealed," must give way to devastating heat and burning desert winds. Only the valley of the Jordan is perennially green; through it flows the largest river of the land which in its north-south course is scarcely one hundred miles long. It plunges some 1,300 feet below sea level and empties into the Dead Sea—the world's lowest and saltiest body of water—ringed around with rocky, barren cliffs.

Because it is so much below the sea level, the Jordan valley is extremely hot. Out of this valley, westward, rises the hill country, where some peaks raise their heads as high as 3,000 feet, but where the average elevation is somewhat less than half that height. Further

13

west, as they meet the Mediterranean, the hills level off into a coastal plain that is no more than twenty miles wide. This plain extends from south to north and breaks off where Mount Carmel, with dramatic suddenness, juts brusquely out to sea, rearing its crest proudly to a height of 1,800 feet and dominating the stately, spacious bay we know today as the Bay of Haifa. At this spot, with Mount Carmel as a sort of pivot, the coastal plain swings sharply inland and, watered by the River Kishon, thrusts its way as far eastward as the Jordan valley. This is the Emek—the valley of Jezreel—today the most fertile part of the country.

This land, once known as Canaan, is now called Palestine, although for Jews it is ever Eretz Israel. In earliest antiquity it formed the principal military highway and trade route that connected the two great river valleys of the Nile on the one hand and the Tigris-Euphrates on the other. Originally it was inhabited by various Canaanitish peoples of Semitic stock, among whom were the Phoenicians and those whom the Egyptians knew as the Amorites. Subsequently the country experienced the influx of the Hittites, then the Arameans and the Hebrews. The Arameans came from that section of the Tigris-Euphrates valley known as Aram-Naharayim (i.e., Aram of the Two Rivers); the Hebrews, from the Sinai peninsula. It was the Hebrews who finally became masters of the land whose historic significance lay in being the more than thousand year bridge between the Empire of the Cuneiform (Babylonia-Assyria) and the Empire of the Hieroglyphs (Egypt). The eyes of the great world empires were constantly focused on this little land, whose role in the great events of antiquity was to be in inverse proportion to its insignificant size.

Into this land settled by Semitic peoples who hailed from the Arabian peninsula there wandered, according to Biblical tradition, a nomad Aramean who four thousand years ago came thither from the north, from Ur of the Chaldees. His name was Abraham and he is reckoned as the progenitor of that people that is known as the people of Israel—the Jewish people—whose story will be told in the succeeding pages. It cannot be gainsaid (no matter what one's attitude to the historical accuracy of the Biblical narrative) that the adventures of Abraham and his immediate descendants, the patriarchs, are echoes of an historical reality and mirror the real events of ancient times much better and more dramatically than many a vague inscription or dust-ridden archaeological discovery. The parting of Lot from Abraham, of Ishmael from Isaac, of Esau from Jacob, reflected the ancient break-up of an aboriginal unity of peoples and remained indelibly impressed upon the folk memory. And when it is always the elder who must give way to the younger, when Ishmael the handmaiden's son is driven away, when the uncouth hunter Esau yields his birthright and father's blessing to the younger, tenderer Jacob, when the young Joseph who bears not only his father's love but visibly God's approval, despite temporary hardships in Egypt, comes into his own and triumphantly asserts himself, then not only the believer, but the historian as well can recognize and confirm the inner truth of this inevitable pattern.

Here we see the great process of a tribe's growth and development embodied in a magnificent saga. We see its will to creative survival emerge stronger and stronger by a process of shedding and casting aside elements at odds with its fundamental direction. Finally we witness its growth to a full-statured peoplehood charged with a world-historic destiny. And when we discover that this development has been indelibly stamped by the personality of the progenitor of the people, Abraham, with his unyielding affirmation of faith, for the first time in history, in the one, true, invisible God, even if it demand the supreme sacrifice, it matters little if skepticism terms such a personality mythical and scoffs at the historical fact of his existence. A clear insight into this spiritual evolution leads to the recognition of the fact that it was an historical reality emerging out of the dim mists of the earliest antiquity rather than the invention of a later culture. As the door slowly swung shut upon this hazy past, the spiritual die had already been cast for the fashioning of a people.

2

The Beginnings of the People

With a company of seventy souls the patriarch Jacob journeyed to Egypt and "there became a great nation." The Biblical record tells us that four hundred and thirty years later (about 1250 B.C.E.) Israel departed from Egypt as a nation of 600,000. These four hundred and thirty years must be taken as a round number symbolizing the span of Israel's slavery in Egypt. Historically, then, these years are as a vacuum, and only at the end of this period does this vacuum begin to be filled, when there was born the man who was destined to be both the builder and teacher of his people—the man Moses.

The personality and achievements of Moses can only be explained against the background of the despotism of the Egyptian Pharaohs, of which the slavery of the Children of Israel was only a reflection. From this background derived that unbounded love not only for his own suffering people, but for all men; from this background, his indestructible faith in the freedom of the individual and in social justice. The nature of his work was threefold, symbolized in the Bible by Exodus, Sinai, Wilderness. Moses became three things all in one—the Emancipator, the Lawgiver, and the Teacher of his people. And so profoundly is the seal of his personality engraved upon his people, that to this very day this threefold influence is preserved in the folk memory

in the form of three great historic-religious festivals—
Pesaḥ, Shavuot and Sukkot. Indeed, Moses proclaimed
them, once and for all, as the very foundations of all
human morality—freedom, law, education.

To put it another way—the exodus from Egypt
made the Children of Israel a nation. The revelation at
Sinai gave them Law. The forty-year sojourn in the wilderness gave the people time to learn the Law and transformed a rabble of slaves into a People of God. It was
then that Moses fashioned that unity of people and religion which is unique in the history of religion and
which is the great secret of Israel's survival.

The central idea behind the Law which Moses
received at Sinai is the unbreakable link between Man,
Nation and Land on the one hand, and God as Lord and
Master of the three, on the other. Just as Man has his
Day of God—the Sabbath—so too the Land has its Year
of God—the Sabbatical Year. This Sabbatical Year,
which serves also as a year of release, makes its influence felt upon the social life, too. The idea of freedom
that emerges from this Law is based squarely upon the
idea of God's People on God's Land. God's bondsman
may not be man's bondsman. This accounts for the revolutionary modification of slavery that we find in the
Mosaic Law which forbids perpetual slavery, limiting it
to six years only, after which the slave must be freed.
Whoever inhabits God's land is only God's tenant
thereon; the soil is holy and inalienable—it must for all
time remain the clan's possession. It explains the Law
of the Year of Jubilee, which recurred every fifty years
to set aright the divine social order that in the interim
had been disturbed. For in that year, "freedom was proclaimed" over Soil, Land and Man. Out of this law
stemmed the protection of the poor and the weak, equal-

ity for stranger and native alike, and insistence upon justice, honest weights and measures and righteous boundaries. Everything was linked to God; every earthly duty was a duty to God and therefore holy; and every action and deed of this world rested upon that sense of obedience which was proclaimed as the loftiest religious duty. And in Judaism it has remained so to this very day.

"Ye shall be holy; for I, the Lord your God, am holy" (Leviticus 19:2). When Moses, for the first time in human history, linked together his teaching of the holiness of God with the sanctification of the everyday, personal, social life of the individual in the spirit of God, when he handed on to the people, not only the Sabbath but also the body of Ritual and Ceremonial Law as the means of educating and training the people, he achieved that great synthesis between Heaven and Earth, Soul and Body, Spirit and Matter, which Israel not merely proclaimed but *lived* as the ultimate religious truth and highest ethical goal. For Moses and for his people, this, then, was the Alpha and the Omega of the revelation at Sinai which the one, holy God brought down into the world as ethical ideal, and the finest of human striving soaring up to the God of heavenly and earthly justice.

That was the Law. What of the man who brought it to the people as God's messenger, and who acted as leader and teacher for forty long years of wandering in the desert? Humility was his most outstanding characteristic and it shines clearly and undeniably through the mists of the three thousand years that separate him from us. No golden-tongued speaker nor eloquent orator was he. In this respect he yielded his place to his brother Aaron whom he appointed to be both high priest and his spokesman. All the events of his personal life bear witness to this humility. "Not I but my people!" was his cry.

And if one may look behind the decisions of God for evidences of man's free will, then one can find it in the magnificent blossoming of a moving renunciation at the very end of his life. Not for him the Promised Land which he, dying, sees but may not enter. Not for him a known grave. He withdraws from the mortal scene behind the eternal shadows of the cliffs and canyons of the Pisgah Hills to die alone, as he had lived—alone and not understood by his people.

3

Travail in the Land of Promise

Soon after Moses died, the invasion of the Hebrews into the Promised Land began. The hostile border tribes of Edom, Moab and Ammon rendered an approach through the south impossible, and so they were compelled to make a wide swing around these territories and enter from the east. They crossed the Jordan under the leadership of Moses' successor, the courageous and capable Joshua. When the fortress of Jericho, that gateway to the ford across the Jordan, fell, the entire land of Canaan rose in determined resistance. The kings of the south mobilized their hosts at Gibeon. After a terrible battle that lasted far into the night, the victory went to Joshua and Israel, and the entire southern part of the country fell into their hands. The Ark of the Covenant was brought northward, and was placed in Shiloh which now served as the center of their worship. The people of the north then resolved to force a decision, but were compelled to yield to the onslaught of the attacker near the source of the Jordan, by the waters of Merom.

However, the entire land was still far from being conquered, nor did the original inhabitants disappear. For the most part, with the exception of those—and they were few—who had been driven to the coast, the Canaanites just remained where they were, living among the Israelites. The one group adapted itself to the other as well as possible, and became more or less accustomed to the new situation. Even before the cross-

21

ing of the Jordan, of all the twelve tribes, just the tribes of Reuben, Gad and part of Manassah requested and received their portion in the Transjordan regions. Thither they betook themselves after the conquest when the land was subdued and divided up.

The continued intermingling between the tribes of Israel and Canaan and their further close contacts with one another inevitably resulted in the condition described in the Book of Judges. The constant refrain which tells us that "The children of Israel deserted God, and God handed them over to . . ." mirrors clearly the clash of cultures that was involved. When we see further that, during those two centuries, individual tribes and not the nation as a whole were affected, it becomes evident how little consolidation and centralization had as yet taken place. The "Judges" who then appeared on the scene, were, indeed, rough and ready warrior heroes—and something more. They did not, all of them, summon the people back to God. When, for example, a leader like Gideon did, we observe that the entire struggle was something more than a tribal conflict—it was a conflict of civilizations, a clash of cultures.

The most dangerous moment of this period came as the entire Canaanitish north rallied round the leadership of the mighty Sisera in order to try to turn the tables on Israel. It took the woman Deborah and the young warrior Barak to defeat Sisera, at the banks of the River Kishon, and there he lost his life in a vain effort to escape. The "Song of Deborah" (Judges 5), one of the most stirring sections of our Bible, paints vividly those turbulent times in the days of the Judges. With bold, broad strokes it depicts the tribes of Israel in their hour of greatest peril, in all their weakness and disorder, but also in their hour of triumph.

4

From Tribe to Kingdom

The men of insight in Israel, and among them the members of the priesthood in Shiloh, saw clearly that a strong centralization of power was the only effective way of meeting the divisive and chaotic condition of the tribal organization. The man who undertook the task of carrying this out was the "seer" Samuel who had been brought up and educated in the circle of the priesthood of Shiloh and who was now its influential leader. To him this was a God-ordained and God-sanctioned task. He had already been the people's leader and judge for many years, when, toward the end of his days, he anointed as king the tall, young, strapping peasant lad of the tribe of Benjamin. Saul it was who for the first time succeeded in uniting all the tribes in a military preemptive strike against the Ammonites across the Jordan. Upon his triumphant return home he became the first King of Israel. The Philistine city-states on Palestine's southern coast, by this time a considerable power, were a constant thorn in his side. His entire reign was spent in conflict with them, and when he fell in battle against them at the foot of the slopes of Gilboa, it looked as though the entire life's effort of that unhappy king had been in vain. But there now came upon the scene that redheaded Judean, stalwart David of the house of Jesse. David, who had won his spurs in the Philistine campaigns, took the reigns of power in his hands and, with a combination of brilliance and ruthlessness, carried through the work of Saul to a successful completion.

The principal contribution of the peasant king Saul was the consolidation of the tribes into a monarchy. David (c. 1000–970 B.C.E.) completed this process and perfected the centralization of the kingdom. Triumphant conquests on all sides extended the boundaries of his empire and gave to his rule an aura of grandeur and brilliance. His greatest achievement, however, lay in moving the capital of the kingdom from Hebron to the newly conquered Jerusalem. He built up this city, which has ever since been associated with his name, as a magnificent center for the monarchy, and it acted as that necessary and effective centralizing force which the country had hitherto lacked. It is with good reason that this period, despite the many human weaknesses of its truly great king, is called the Golden Age of the Kingdom of Israel. Striking proof of what his memory meant to the people can be found in the fact that the authorship of the entire Book of Psalms, that great treasure store of ancient Jewish piety and religiosity, is attributed to him. This, despite the fact that his authorship of all the Psalms is by no means established, indicates how the people idealized their king. Indeed, for all time David remained in the eyes of Israel as the royal hero and singer. All the hopes and longings of the people have attached themselves to his name to this very day.

His son Solomon (c. 970–950 B.C.E.) completed his father's work by erecting a suitable abode for the divine presence. David himself had brought the Ark of the Covenant into his new capital, but it was not given to him to build a fitting structure to house it. It was in Solomon's reign that the magnificent Temple was constructed. Solomon also undertook a lavish program of public works. All this required of the people the heaviest taxes, both in money and in forced labor, and a strong popular dissatisfaction with his reign began to make itself felt. Furthermore Solomon, who had among his many wives a daughter of the Pharaohs, modeled his rule after them, built palace after palace and thrust an ever heavier yoke upon his people. So the ground was prepared for the fierce revolt which broke out shortly after his death. It was led by the energetic steward Jeroboam, and Solomon's young son and successor was quite unable to cope with it. The ten tribes in the north under the leadership of Jeroboam seceded from the union and set up an independent state, and only the royal tribe of Judah was left to the House of David. Despite this unhappy ending, Solomon's was indeed a brilliant and colorful reign. There had been an era of peace. Trade and commerce flourished. National prestige was high and it was buttressed by favorable foreign treaties. Ships that plied back and forth to distant climes from the Red Sea ports brought to Israel the wonders of distant lands, and to those lands in return they brought the beauties of Israel. And Solomon, despite his many failings, was, like his father, a very capable and effective ruler, and a just judge to his people. In popular legend and proverb he has remained the symbol of learning, erudition and wisdom.

5

Between Two Empires

Now there were two kingdoms, the North and the South. The northern kingdom of Israel, though larger and politically more powerful, was the more unstable because it suffered from a constant series of violent changes of dynasties. The southern kingdom of Judah, tiny and politically impotent, possessed the holy city of Jerusalem and the enduring Davidic dynasty which gave it a greater degree of stability, and, in the end, a longer history.

The history and final decline of these two states can best be understood against the background of the mighty world events as they unfolded themselves in the whole of the Middle East, between the ninth and sixth centuries of the pre-Christian era. Israel and Judah were situated between the two great empires of ancient times, the Empire of the Nile (land of the hieroglyphs) on the one hand, and the Empire of the Tigris-Euphrates (land of the cuneiform) on the other. It was the destiny of these two little lands to be literally squeezed out of existence by the tremendous three-century struggle for control of the Middle East by these two great empires. Israel and Judah formed the key portions of the land bridge that linked Asia with Africa, and were consequently the route of march for the Egyptian and Chaldean armies. Whoever held Palestine held the key to the approach to each of these continents. Therefore it was an all-important part of Egyptian, then Assyrian, and later Babylonian strategy to win and hold control of this little land. It is the ebb and flow of these conflicting major interests mirrored in the vacillating policies of the "pigmy" kings of Jerusalem and Samaria which, despite the constant warnings of their prophets, resulted in final disaster for both them and their countries.

In the ninth century, Assyria still represented only a veiled and distant threat against Israel. Between them stood the buffer state Aram (Syria), which for a century was Israel's archenemy. After constant struggle, the country won a respite under the leadership of King Omri (about 800 B.C.E.), who built the city of Samaria as the national capital and therewith gave the country its center. Next to it, Jezreel, in the northern valley, served as an auxiliary seat of the monarchy. Omri was succeeded by his able son Ahab (about 860) who is best known for the fact that it was during his reign that the prophet Elijah lived and flourished. He was able to hold back the Arameans, and his reign saw the beginnings of a boom in trade and commerce. But this was again interrupted by a violent dynastic change. Jehu, a daring soldier, led the officers in a revolt that placed him on the throne. Among the victims of the revolt were Ahab's successor, Joram, the Queen Mother Jezebel and all their court. That was the "bloody day of Jezreel" of which later prophets spoke so ominously.

Not long after, something similar happened in Jerusalem. Ahab's daughter, Athalia, widow of the Judean king Joram, attempted to extirpate the entire dynasty and caused the murder of her own children. The youngest son, Joash, was rescued by the priests. When he grew a little older, Athalia herself was killed in an army revolt planned by the high priest and Joash succeeded to the throne.

Thus these two little kingdoms trembled under the dual impact of world-shaking events from without and violent dynastic changes from within. However, the northern kingdom enjoyed another period of prosperity during the reign of Jeroboam II (about 760), a great-grandson of Jehu's. But once again there followed dynastic changes and civil war, which rendered the country all the weaker and more powerless in the face of the impending onslaught of Assyria. Tiglat Pileser plundered the land, and his successor Shalmanesser destroyed the state. Samaria fell in 722 after a three-year siege that was led by the general Sargon, and in keeping with the Assyrian policy of depopulating conquered provinces, the great portion of the people were led into exile. Thus it was that the Ten Tribes disappeared from the stage of history into the melting pot of peoples in the growing empire of Assyria. Judah and Jerusalem remained.

But this was just a temporary reprieve, even though the southern kingdom lived for another century and a half on borrowed time. The fate of the Middle East was sealed. Still Assyria-Nineveh stood at the peak of her power, though this power was soon to be usurped completely by Babylon. In addition to this the Scythians threatened from the north and swept down like locusts over the plains of Asia. Toward the end of the seventh century Egypt stirred once more. The last powerful Pharaoh, Necho by name, attempted to take advantage of the momentary confusion in the north caused principally by the sudden collapse of Nineveh and the equally sudden emergence of Babylon, by again asserting Egypt's claims to world domination. In the year 608 he attacked suddenly and hurled his forces against the north. At Megiddo he found himself opposed by Josiah, king of Judah, who had become allied with Babylonia, and in the ensuing battle this young monarch lost his life. But Pharaoh Necho had miscalculated. For Nebuchadnezzar, the up-and-coming king of Babylonia, had succeeded in overthrowing Nineveh completely in the year 606. And when Necho and his hosts reached the upper waters of the Euphrates, they found that Nebuchadnezzar and his cohorts were quite ready for them, and Egypt sustained a shattering defeat.

With this battle the fate of the world was determined. Babylonia was victorious. Egypt was vanquished. And Judah fell prostrate under the heel of the victor. But Egypt refused to submit and by constant intrigues and promises attempted to stir up disaffection in Jerusalem. A new revolt broke out against Babylonia, nurtured by the fanatic love of liberty in a people moved by the startling course of events. This resulted first of all in a punitive expedition and the deportation of King Jehoiachin together with many of the leaders of the people (597). When this did not prove completely effective, Nebuchadnezzar returned for a second visit in the year 586 and completely destroyed Judah. On the ninth day of Ab Jerusalem was conquered and destroyed, the Temple was burnt to the ground, and the last king, Zedekiah, was blinded and led with the greater part of his people into Babylonian exile.

6

The Voice of Prophecy

Thus Judah, a century and a half later, met Israel's fate. However, the three-century story of the divided kingdoms of Israel and Judah might have been the insignificant story of two tiny peoples, had it not brought forth one of the most glorious phenomena in the realm of ancient history—the prophecy of Israel.

The soil that Moses planted, though oft-threatened by Canaanitish paganism, and profoundly furrowed by the plow of the great world events of the day, bore its fruit at last and bore it a hundred-fold. The prophets as we know them emerged from an ancient religious guild whose members were possessed of strange manner, mien and voice, and were looked upon by the people as being on the queer side. They came to their full stature and development in those great personalities who stepped out of the confines of the guild and became the religious and moral opposition of their time. We call them the major and minor prophets according to the number of their utterances which have come down to us. In telling their story much of what has gone before is recapitulated, omitting the review of external events while probing beneath the surface for inner examination and evaluation.

Moses was in spirit the father of the prophetic movement. In the seer Samuel, who anointed Saul as king, we see a distinct reawakening of this prophetic strain. It came to life with fullest force in the powerful and meteoric appearance of Elijah, who, around the year 870 B.C.E. emerges as the opponent of King Ahab who had succeeded in turning back the Syrian menace. This solitary prophet was a man of tough and granite-like single-mindedness. With unbending determination and unyielding stubbornness he fought the cult of Baal which the Phoenician-born Queen Jezebel had tried to introduce into the country. He was devoted with a passionate attachment and clear understanding to his great predecessor Moses, and battled against the alien cult with fire and sword. Singlehanded he fought the battle of God, and only later in his career, when most of his work was done, was he joined by his successor Elisha, who was more his servant than his disciple.

The first of what we call the literary prophets—those who spoke and wrote down their own utterances—was that herdsman from the Judean hill country, Amos of Tekoah. Around the year 760 B.C.E. he crossed the frontier into Israel, and came to the religious center at Bethel. There it was that during the Autumn Festival he appeared and smote the altar with his staff so that the pillars shook. This happened during the reign of Jeroboam II, a period of great material prosperity that was but a thin mask covering the social rottenness at its core. By calling for justice for the first time since Moses, Amos returned to the social challenges of the Mosaic Law and proved himself the true disciple of his master. His battle against the prevailing cult, its sacrifices and priesthood, was not aimed at eliminating them. Rather was it against the point of view that identified religion solely with external observances divorced from the obligation of morality, justice and righteousness in everyday social life. He was not opposed to outward form, but to empty formalism. He was not opposed to priesthood, but to a vision-blunted priesthood preoccupied solely with the outward panoplies of a ritualistic cult. Thus he became the father of all later prophets. What to him was the difference between priest and prophet as persons became to his followers a contrast between the principles of priesthood and prophecy.

Twenty years later there came on the scene as the first of these followers the unhappy prophet Hosea. The tragedy of his personal, domestic life became transmuted, and from his pain-scarred lips the call of social justice of the blunt herdsman of Tekoah was transformed into the cry of longing of God's love for Israel. This movement grew to its fullest stature in the person of the great prophet Isaiah whom fate placed in the very midst of the decline of the kingdom of Israel (725–700 B.C.E.), whose collapse he witnessed from Jerusalem. It was he who helped Judah avoid a similar fate at that time, and he was able to do so because he combined within himself statesmanship and prophecy. Not only was he a genuine follower of Amos the shepherd in summoning the people to follow the path of justice and loyalty, not only did he, in his public appearance, in the matchless rhythm and power of his speech, interpret the great world events of his time as God acting through history, not only was he the first with outstretched hand to point to the vision of a messianic age over the horizon, but in his role as an influential courtier, standing close to the throne, he was able to impress this point of view strongly and effectively upon state policy.

The age was wild and unbridled; the powers of political seduction and allurement were great. In that decisive hour, when in the year 701 the Chaldean hosts were encamped at the very gates of Jerusalem and surrender seemed inevitable, it was Isaiah who prevented it. When the Chaldeans, owing to the twin hammer-strokes of a plague in their ranks and threats of revolt at home, were compelled to withdraw as suddenly as they had appeared, Isaiah, standing at the side of the noble King Hezekiah, found himself the hero of the hour. Above all else, this miraculous turn of events engraved upon the hearts of the people an unswerving faith in the inviolability of the Mount of the Temple. This firm faith, degenerating into smugness in the following century, became a dangerous narcotic.

It was against the current of this belief-become-smugness, raised to fever pitch by a patriotic fanaticism, that the last of the great prophets of Judah, Jeremiah of Anatoth, struggled fervently with an aching heart. He was at once the most personal and the most tragic of the prophets of Israel. He saw the evil and proclaimed it. He battled against the vain illusions of the masses, but no one listened to him. Scorned by the priests, pilloried by the people, he suffered imprisonment first in a slimy mud pit, and then in the Temple. Still he battled on. Only once, after the Scythian menace had suddenly vanished, did there appear the faintest flicker of hope for the success of his efforts. The rediscovery in 621, of that long-forgotten fifth book of Moses, the so-called Book of Deuteronomy, was the direct cause of a great wave of religious reform under the rule of the young King Josiah. He it was who fell in battle at Megiddo some years later. In this housecleaning, the last remnants of Canaanitish paganism were rooted out, and it appeared as though a new era for religion and morality was in the offing. But it was too late. The mad whirlpool of a world in upheaval was dragging all with it into its vortex. The tornado swept over Asia. Nineveh tottered and fell (606).

Egypt went under (604). Mighty Babylon surged to the surface and finally emerged victorious as the ruler of all Asia. All the while, political terror and patriotic frenzy raged in Jerusalem. Thus the Holy City fell at last in 586 B.C.E., and it remained for Jeremiah, who perhaps loved his people in its suffering with a greater passion and intensity than anyone since Moses, to sing its elegy, preserved in Lamentations. In spite of all this, he never gave up hope. With the very end in sight, while he himself was still imprisoned, he gave tangible proof of his faith in the future by purchasing a new plot of ground. And after the destruction he was among the first to give succor to the poor and bedraggled remnant in the ruined land. The difficult task was placed in the hands of the governor Gedaliah, whom Jeremiah joined. But Gedaliah was murdered by a fanatic who opposed him politically and who, oddly, bore the un-Judean name of Ishmael. The last group of leaders, fearing Babylonian reprisals, fled to Egypt and compelled Jeremiah to flee with them. There we lose all sight of this great prophet and there, in all likelihood, he died.

7

By the Waters of Babylon

The period of Babylonian exile is the decisive turning point in the history of the Jewish people. To Babylon
in the wake of the exiles there went, side by side, the
coffin of the nation and the cradle of Judaism. Unlike
their brothers the Ten Lost Tribes, the exiles from
Judah have survived. That they were able to was in no
small measure due to those two great prophets who
arose, the one at the beginning, the other at the end of
the period of exile. The one was Ezekiel, the other, Deutero-Isaiah (Isaiah 40–66). Like two mighty pillars it is
they who bear the arch of those fifty years.

Ezekiel was a priest who had been among the exiles
of 597. It was with comfort and confidence that he
greeted the vast body of those who followed in 586. He
was always the priest both in speech and in thought. His
imagery was drawn from the cult (Chap. 1), his style
from theology. He grappled with the problems of Israel
and Judah on an almost strictly dogmatic plane of
morality whose key was to be found in the idea of guilt
and expiation. But his viewpoint was vigorous enough
to reawaken a strong flicker of hope in the hearts of the
people (Chap. 18). If prophecy's former task was to fight
against vain illusions, it now had to struggle against the
spirit of despair and hopelessness that dissolved in tears
by the waters of Babylon (Chap. 37 and Psalm 137).
Ezekiel the priest-prophet, made himself the herald of

a national revival and taught the exiles to consider their present plight simply as a period of transition that would have to be overcome.

It was, however, more than a mere period of transition. It was first of all a sort of religious vacuum. The exiles had been uprooted from their religious as well as national soil. The Temple was in ruins, sacrifices had ceased. The idle priests were as aimless as officers of a defeated army. Gradually there came about an incisive change not only in convictions, but also in religious forms. Exactly how, when or where it happened we do not know. However, on the basis of historical evidence we must assume that during those fifty years the people created the institution of the synagogue as a substitute for the lost Temple worship. Prayer took the place of sacrifice. The Sabbath, until then only a day of rest, became a day of assembly, and in the House of Assembly—the Synagogue—the Book was placed upon the table, instead of the sacrifice upon the altar. Therein is to be found the roots of the worship of the Book which for thousands of years was to leave its impress upon Israel's countenance. Therein are to be found the roots of that liturgy which to this day is characteristic of what it lacks and longs for. It arose as a substitute for the Temple worship that was lost. It became and has remained to this day the bearer of a tremulous longing and a constancy of faith. The art of writing spread. The first scribes were priests, but soon the whole people was swept away and the scribe began to supersede the priest. This period, in truth, was the hour of birth of Judaism.

In the meantime events stirred once more in Asia. After the strong and lengthy reign of Nebuchadnezzar, Babylon began to totter. Cyrus the Persian came upon the scene, mastered Media, overthrew Lydia, gained control of Asia Minor, and it was only a question of time as to Babylon's turn. During those crucial days, about the year 540, there arose among the exiles the anonymous prophet who is responsible for the last twenty-seven chapters of the Book of Isaiah and a few other parts of it. We know him therefore as Deutero-Isaiah or the Second Isaiah. He towers above the other prophets by virtue of his lofty style which most powerfully expressed the mood of the exiles. It was in hymns that he proclaimed the coming of God, the great God of the world, in whose eyes all the nations of the world were but as a tiny droplet in a vast sea. It was in hymns too that he greeted Cyrus as the messenger, indeed as the messiah appointed by God for the task of restoring Israel to his ancient glory. His first word was comfort, his last—promise. When, finally, he pictured Israel as the suffering servant of God, bearing on his shoulders the sins of others (Chap. 53), he tore the veil from the mystery of the events of the past fifty years and showed how God worked through history and through time.

In the year 538 Cyrus entered Babylon in triumph. Soon after he gave the exiles permission to return home.

8

Homecoming and Rebuilding

Only a portion of the exiles returned home in the year 537. They were led by a priest and a prince, Joshua and Zerubabel. The beautiful one hundred and twenty-sixth Psalm magnificently depicts the emotions of the pilgrims who, accompanied by the blessings and the gifts of those they left behind, returned as though in a happy dream. They found the land overrun on all sides by strangers. To the north were the Samaritans, a conglomeration of the remnants of the debacle of 722 and alien settlers who had been brought in by the Assyrians. The west, east and south had been invaded by the neighboring peoples. The returning exiles settled in and around Jerusalem and at once set up the altar anew. Twenty years passed before the Temple was completed, twenty years filled with hardship and struggle principally because of the bitter hostility and enmity of the Samaritans. At last, in spite of all the obstacles, Joshua and Zerubabel, aided by the prophets Haggai and Zechariah, succeeded in bringing the reconstruction of the Temple to a successful conclusion by the year 516. This enormously strengthened the backbone and morale of the settlers, but their troubles were by no means over. Indeed, as the years passed they increased. Reinforcements from Babylonia were meager. The threat of disintegration by intermarriage with the strangers grew greater.

Things had indeed gone so far by the year 469 that in the eyes of the pious, salvation could only come from Babylonia. And come it did, in the person of the priest and scribe Ezra, who appeared on the scene in Jerusalem in the year 456. With an unbending energy he lost no time in coming to grips with the situation. He strove to prevent the spread of mixed marriages, but despite some external success he was unable at once to strike at the roots of the evil. Somewhat more successful was Nehemiah, who had been a favorite courtier of King Artaxerxes. He came to Jerusalem a little later and concluded that it would be much easier to concentrate upon strengthening the city of Jerusalem before trying to settle the land as a whole. With this in view he swiftly pushed to completion the construction of a wall around Jerusalem, much to the chagrin of all the neighboring enemies of the Jews. Then began the process of resettling every tenth Jew from the surrounding country in the city. This gave the city a more substantial population and made it a stronger economic force. For now both city and market were in the hands of the Jews, and trade and commerce could be controlled in their best interests. It was also possible for him to make proper allowances for the observance of the Sabbath, to regulate the still unorganized priestly affairs, and to carry forward Ezra's campaign against intermarriage.

With Ezra's return to Jerusalem some years later, the two leaders, in close cooperation, were able to crown their efforts with success. The year 444 marks one of the most decisive events in the history of the Jewish people. For in that year, within the Temple confines, the entire people and their representatives in solemn oath reaffirmed their allegiance to the Mosaic Code. This climaxed the great return—which was born in Babylonia and which resulted in a reconstructed Judaism replanted in its native soil. The Temple service was once again placed in the hands of the priests, but something new had happened. The new faith was based, not as formerly upon the cult, but upon the Law. Side by side with the Temple there now stood in equal rank both House of Study and Synagogue. The teacher of the Law had a status equal with that of the priest. The Law was the Law of God, revealed at Sinai and handed down through the ages.

9

The Age of Hellenism

In the space of three centuries Israel had witnessed the rise and fall of world empires, had experienced destruction and exile twice—and still lived on. To the amazement of an incredulous world, the nation raised its head again and seemed to be able to carry on more firmly than ever. The rest of the Persian period (440–330) was, for the Jewish people, a period of further consolidation. The Temple cult, with its Levites and singers, developed strongly. The Synagogue, with its regular cycle of Torah reading and liturgy, took form and thrived. The study of Torah (Midrash) flourished. The high priest became titular head of the people. His was no meager power and events pointed toward the development of an enduring theocracy. The priests took up the study of Torah with great zeal. Under their guidance it became the duty of all to learn to read and write. The literature was cultivated and developed. A greater emphasis than ever was placed upon the Hebrew language, since during the course of the Exile the Aramaic tongue had become the vernacular of the bulk of the people. To be sure it was even necessary to translate the Torah into this vernacular (Targum). At the same time, with ever greater energy the ancient cultural treasures of historical, prophetic and poetic books were gathered, to form the backbone of the later Biblical canon.

Here it is necessary once more to mention the Book of Psalms. Just as the Torah (Pentateuch) and the Prophets are the great religious documents of pre-exilic Israel, so the Psalms are the great document of Judaism in its early post-exilic stage. To be sure the psalm-form was the creation of an earlier day and its origins could be traced back to King David himself. However, in its totality, this great collection of religious poetry and song was the product not of the people of the First Temple, but of the People of the Book. The manifold attempts to stamp the spirit of Ezra and his followers as the hardening of Israel's religious arteries, in contrast to the warm soaring genius of the prophets, fall to the ground when we consider the Psalms in this light. The spirit of the Law, which became ever stronger and stronger, was in fullest harmony with the genuine piety, fervor and longing after God which are the basic themes of the great symphony that forms the Book of Psalms. And this Book accompanied the Jew on his journey through the centuries not simply as the great hymnal of the Second Temple, but as his most faithful treasure.

This much must be made clear. The religious thinking and feeling of the period of the Second Temple do not represent a retrogression from the prophetic peaks. Rather do they represent a new orientation, and in some respects even an advance. No longer is it simply the nation; it is the community, recognized by all as the bearer, spiritually and morally, of a common possession. The nation now felt itself a community, and the Psalms that resounded in the Temple gave a powerful expression to the profundity and depth of this feeling.

There appeared at this stage, too, the books of wisdom literature—Proverbs, Ecclesiastes and Ben Sirach. Originating during the Greek period, these books became a body of literature, whose popularity among the people bore witness to the moral attitude of the masses as well as to the common sense and simplicity of the new community. The fact that this ancient Jewish wisdom with its moral strength and power of simile was able to win its way into the treasury of world proverbs is sufficient testimony to the high quality of the youthful Judaism of that period (300–100 B.C.E.).

But perhaps more than all the rest, it is the Book of Job, with its profundity and intensity, that gives the clearest evidence of the glory and greatness of Jewish literary creativity of that age. Tradition ascribes the authorship of the book to Moses. The exact date of its creation is by no means certain, but the nature of the religious problem that is posed seems to point to a relatively late period. Its central problem is the relationship between human suffering and guilt. The masterly treatment of this problem, the revolt of Job against the narrow-minded, smug point of view that accepts all human suffering as an evidence of human guilt, and the continued faith in God and longing after God on the part of the innocent sufferer, despite all—these are factors that make the book the finest fruit of all the literature of this period. Above all else, it is an indisputable fact that the Bible remains indebted to the period of the Scribes and possibly even to that of the Pharisees for this book, which takes its honored place close to the Pentateuch.

While the first lovely bloom of this period was unfolding, the world was shaken to its very foundations by another great revolution. This time the storm came from the west and put all else in the shade. By the year 480, at the Battle of Salamis, the great Persian Empire, reaching westward in its world-conquering impetus, received its first rebuff at the hands of the Greeks. The

Occident, with Alexander as its propelling force, swept through the Orient like a hurricane, and for the third time since Assyria-Babylonia, Israel experienced a tremendous world upheaval. In the year 333 Alexander won the battle of Issus, and the whole world lay at his triumphant feet. In Jewish legend he appears in an aura compounded of affection and gratitude. Jewish children were named after him. The age of the learned high priest Simon the Just, and of his followers the Men of the Great Assembly, reverberates with his fame and glory.

But for decades after Alexander's premature death the world was torn by the strife of successors who tried in vain to assume his mantle. Once again little Judea became the political football of warring interests. When an exhausted Asia finally found a temporary respite, an ancient pattern began to weave itself again. Once more Judea found itself between two contending empires. In Egypt, center of the African portion of Alexander's Empire, the Ptolemies held sway with their capital in the great metropolis of Alexandria. In the north, the center of gravity of Assyrian-Babylonian suzerainty shifted to Syria, where the Seleucid kings set up their authority in the city of Antioch. The Ptolemies maintained their control over Judea until the year 200, with the high priests in Jerusalem as their tributary rulers.

The march of Hellenism with its new world of gods and culture was a tremendous experience for the young Judaism. It swept into the ken of the national experience of the Jew, bearing in its hands both blessing and curse. The greatness of the experience contained within it the greatness of the peril. Almost in the twinkling of an eye the Jews of Judea were confronted with another great diaspora alongside the numerous Jewish communities of Babylonia—the new, great, growing Jewish community of Egypt. The city of Alexandria contained an enormous Jewish community covering great sections of the city, with its renowned synagogue and its Jews who spoke Greek and bore Greek names, and who were schooled in and greatly influenced by the teachings of Socrates and Plato. The Bible was translated into Greek, tradition has it, by seventy scholars and is called the Septuagint. It had to be translated, for the people in Egypt for the most part no longer understood Hebrew. Indeed, so deep did the roots penetrate into the new environment that there was even a conscious attempt to break with the religious ties that bound them to the motherland. This was the attempt at building a rival temple at Leontopolis, the Temple of Onias. It speaks well for the healthy Jewish instincts of this wing of the dispersion that though this structure was completed, it failed of its purpose. The ancient Temple tax (one-half shekel) still went to Jerusalem, and the Temple remained the center of a Judaism whose bearers were now scattered throughout the length and breadth of the Mediterranean world.

Around the year 200, the Seleucid monarch Antiochus conquered Palestine, and with this conquest begins the fateful Seleucid rule over Judea. It brought in its wake, after many upheavals, that great national and religious revival which is indissolubly linked with the name of the Maccabees. Of the three segments into which Alexander's Empire split up after his death, Asia represented the most serious problem for Hellenism. For here, much more than in relatively unified Egypt, was the herculean task of merging that great confusion of peoples—Syrians, Cilicians, Pontians, Cappodicians, and those as far as the Indus—in the gigantic melting pot of Greek culture and pantheon. A younger Antiochus, surnamed Epiphanes, undertook to give this problem a radical and violent solution, and his grandiose plans of forcible amalgamation were shattered on the tiny reef that was Judea. The victory of the Maccabees sealed his defeat. For Judea itself these wars and victories meant considerably more than the attainment of political autonomy. Up to that time political and cultural leadership had rested in the hands of a priestly aristocracy with its principal support in the capital, Jerusalem. Now the priesthood, demoralized and debauched by an inferior brand of Hellenism, completely forfeited its power and popular respect.

Bitter intrigues and inner conflicts in Jerusalem itself preceded the wars. The masses of the people were outraged by the shameless traffic for the office of high priest that went on in the ante-chambers of the court at Antioch, a traffic in which the candidates stopped at nothing. Assassination, plundering of the Temple to curry favor with Antiochus, the introduction of pagan Grecian customs into the capital, climaxed by the introduction of a statue of the Greek god into the Temple—all this on the part of those who scrambled madly for the position of high priest raised popular resentment to fever pitch. Like an exploding volcano the revolt erupted in the countryside. In the tiny mountain city of Modin, Mattathias, head of the Hasmonean household, a rural priestly family, raised the flag of revolt. Around him and his five sturdy sons the pious and the faithful rallied. Out of the bloodstains of an unparalleled heroic suffering in the face of the religious persecutions of Antiochus, there emerged, as though overnight, the heroes of the struggle. It began with scattered guerrilla warfare in the hills. One success led to another until finally Judas Maccabeus, the third of the five brothers, destroyed the Syrian armies in three major battles at Beth Horon, Emmaus and Beth Zur, captured Jerusalem, cleansed the Temple of Greek idolatry, and reconsecrated it to its ancient service (Chanukah) in the year 165 B.C.E. Once again the strings of the harp of David were stirred and magnificent Psalms resounded proclaiming the great rebirth of those days.

The death of Judas and the death of Antiochus occurred in the same year. The elder Hasmonean brother, Jonathan, was able to make skillful use of dynastic disputes that broke out in Antioch and concluded an honorable peace with the Syrians which assured and recognized Judea's autonomy. But the work of the Maccabees was crowned with final success by another Hasmonean son, Simon, who in the year 141 founded the Hasmonean dynasty by uniting in his person the office of king and high priest. This union of the temporal and spiritual for the time being put an end to party strife. But more important than this was the fact that the final victory of the Maccabees represented the final victory of Judaism over Hellenism. That which was good and worthwhile in Hellenism was usefully absorbed; the dross of its paganism was expelled and cast aside. Thus it was that only tiny Israel could hold its ground and overcome the greatest cultural upheaval of the ancient world. In this marriage of the Orient with the Occident, which was the great vision of Alexander, Judaism took Hellenism as a bride, but itself remained the bridegroom and master. It was a victory woven out of the heroism of battles, and the greater heroism of suffering and persecution.

10

The Roman Eagle

Now began the decline. Much of the blame for this rests upon the shoulders of the new Hasmonean dynasty. True, that dynasty was a product of the soil and was carried along by the tide of religious revolt and exaltation. But now, after kingship and priesthood had been united, the scepter was again in the hands of the old aristocracy. The high priesthood became but a decoration for the princes, and temporal power was supreme.

The rulers embarked upon a policy that swayed perilously between legitimacy and popularity. Worldliness led to moral disintegration. The princes, tearing one another to bits in family squabbles, and venting their spite upon their own people, inevitably played right into the hands of world-conquering Rome, with their unhappy land as pawn.

Even Simon, the first Hasmonean king, fell under the ruthless blow of an assassin—his own son-in-law. Then, after a short period of prosperity and affluence under the rule of Simon's son John Hyrcanus, the family strife began again and blossomed into civil war. Judas Aristobulus threw his own mother and brother into prison; Alexander Jannai ran amok in the Temple itself; a brief breathing spell followed under the rule of his widow, Salome Alexandra. But no sooner had her two sons, Hyrcanus and Aristobulus, grown to maturity, and the worthy queen had breathed her last, than they were at one another's throats. The younger, Aristobulus, sought to usurp his brother's crown, and soon internecine strife was raging. Neighboring peoples took a hand in the struggle and in the year 63 B.C.E. the two brothers finally brought their conflicting claims for arbitration to the Roman conqueror Pompey in Damascus. This was a fatal step so far as Judea's independence was concerned. For now, in the person of Pompey, who had established Rome's mastery over the Orient with his victory over Mithridates in the year 64, Rome laid her heavy hands upon little Judea, never again to raise them.

Pompey took a good look at the two candidates, and decided in favor of the weaker, Hyrcanus. Now all was over for the dynasty. For the only thing that had given its rule any meaning—the attempt to give the land political standing by the force of arms and by treaties—had failed utterly. The despairing attempts to recoup the situation during the confusion of the civil strife in Rome itself went awry. Alexander, the son of Aristobulus, who had escaped the clutches of the Romans, tried it in the year 57 B.C.E. and failed. Seventeen years later, another Hasmonean, Antigonus, tried again. He had a measure of success for three years, but in the year 37 B.C.E. he was superseded by the man who was to guide the destinies of Judea for thirty years, and who was to conquer Jerusalem with Roman aid. That man was Herod. Antigonus was removed by the executioner's axe.

Herod was the son of Antipater, an Idumean. The Idumeans, descendants of the Edomites, were a people dwelling on the southern borders of Judea. A century previous Edom had been conquered by John Hyrcanus and its inhabitants forcibly converted to Judaism. From the day that Pompey judged the claims of the contending brothers, Judea had in effect been ruled by procurators appointed by Rome. The royal and priestly office that Hyrcanus had received at his hands was bereft of all real power. True power rested in the hands of his minister, the Idumean Antipater, the foreigner who had first ingratiated himself as evil spirit into the favor of the weakling Hyrcanus, but who finally, under the mounting drive of his personal ambition, began dealing directly with Rome. Antipater was nothing more than a Roman pawn who knew well how to fawn upon his masters, skillfully hopping from Pompey to Caesar. But in all other respects he was a man of unbending purpose and ruthlessness. He met his death by poisoning, and was succeeded in power by his son Herod.

Herod maneuvered his way to royal position and ruled as a veritable tyrant. He began with a mass execution of all his enemies. He rooted out every member of the Hasmonean family, and even though he began by marrying the Hasmonean princess Mariamne, in order to give his rule an air of legitimacy he had her executed in a fit of madness and jealousy, and his two sons as well. But despite his savage character he did not lack greatness. World destiny once again trembled in the balance in the earth-shaking struggle for power between Anthony and Cleopatra in Egypt and Caesar Octavianus in the west. In this kaleidoscopic situation, Herod showed himself to be a man of lightning-like judgments. Dodging adroitly to and fro between the principal rivals, skillfully evading the constant thrusts of his embittered personal enemies, he managed always to do the right thing at the right time, and he survived the great Battle of Actium (31), retaining his personal power despite all his enemies. This world-decisive battle settled the imperial score in favor of Octavian, who as Roman Emperor became known as Caesar Augustus. When Herod died in the year 4 B.C.E., the virulent hatred of the people he had oppressed followed him to his grave, and it blazed forth in a violent uprising against Rome, whose domination his rule had symbolized to them. Rome and Edom now came to mean the same thing in the eyes of the Jews. This revolt marked the beginning of the end for the Jews in their native Judea.

11

The Pharisees, Sadducees and Essenes

Just as it would be utterly impossible to understand the inner meaning of the two centuries preceding the destruction of the First Temple without a consideration of the significant phenomenon of Jewish prophecy, so too would a complete grasp of what now follows be virtually impossible without taking into account the equally significant phenomenon of Pharisaism. To be sure the latter did not quite equal the former in fiery genius. But as a creative, constructive force within Judaism, it was certainly no less significant. The word Pharisee (Hebr. *Parush,* Aram. *Parish*) means "Separatist." But it does not stand for a sect or party so much as for a program. The Pharisees were the heirs of the pious Assideans (Ḥassidim) who had come into being during the religious persecutions of Antiochus Epiphanes. Even before the Maccabean struggle, at a time when the priestly classes yielded to Hellenism, they formed the vigorous opposition. So too, after the victory, when the Hasmonean dynasty allied itself with the representatives of that same pro-Hellenist priesthood, they withdrew still more and consistently transferred their opposition to the dynasty. Through them, in this struggle against the forces of Hellenism, the people attained a higher degree of self-consciousness and self-determination. If the Maccabees won political autonomy for the people, the Pharisees maintained their spiritual autonomy in the Law and Tradition. A good look at the gods of the Greeks gave to these pious ones a clearer understanding than ever just what Israel was, and why and how it differed from the pagan. More than any of the others, it was they who recognized clearly exactly what a threat Hellenism represented for Judaism. They became separatists, and therefore called themselves "Perushim"—Pharisees.

When their opponents, who originally found their support in the priestly family of the Zadokites, consolidated themselves as the partisans of the Hasmoneans, their family name became the group name of the so-called Sadducees (Zadokim). The influence and power of the Pharisees among the common people grew as their opponents turned aside from religious interests and became absorbed in worldly statecraft. Even the fact that the Hasmoneans were the high priests failed to conceal their primarily temporal interests. The Pharisees with abundant energy pointed to this unpriestly behavior, and their opposition did not stop short of open demonstrations in the Temple itself. To this fact the brutal massacre of many leading Pharisees in the Temple engineered by Alexander Jannai bears bloody testimony.

Judas Maccabeus had raised aloft the banner of revolt not simply for political freedom, but for freedom to observe divine law as well. So too did the program of the Pharisees emphasize the Law as Ezra had reintroduced it. It was quite natural that those who were schooled and learned in the Scriptures became the principal bearers of the Pharisaic idea. They did not seek political or temporal power. They sought power where they felt it would be fruitful, in the synagogue *(bet hak'nesset)*, in the house of study *(bet hamidrash)* and above all in the Sanhedrin. This supreme court of seventy-one members had its seat in Jerusalem and, until then, was controlled by the priestly aristocracy. But now the Pharisees finally attained their goal. The Hasmoneans yielded to their pressure. As a matter of fact, Salome Alexandra, widow of the violent Alexander Jannai, opened wide the doors of the Sanhedrin to them. From that time on the Pharisees formed the immutable rock and immobile pole in the tempestuous period of Roman domination. As representatives of the religious discipline in the synagogue, school and court, they were, in fact, in this period of tragic decline, the true saviors and preservers of Judaism and, through it, of the Jewish people. Their much criticized exclusiveness was in fact the final wisdom of men of the greatest insight in a time of the greatest crisis.

The picture of the Pharisees that we get in the New Testament is misleading because it is tendentious. The Pharisees as such were neither hypocrites nor formalists, as early Christianity has stamped them. Characters like Hillel of Babylon, who in the black days of Herod's rule and during the early lifetime of Jesus was head of the Great Sanhedrin, are clear-cut evidence of the opposite. His humility, patience and genuine love for his fellow men have become by-words far beyond the bounds of Judaism itself. Even his contemporary and opponent in the Sanhedrin, Shammai, a sterner man than Hillel, was such a creative, positive force that the reproaches against this man, and the great school which he, like Hillel, founded, fall to the ground.

There is ample evidence that this was an age supercharged with religious profundity and emotion. For in addition to the Pharisees and Sadducees there was still another group. This was a silent, taciturn group, that broke completely with worldly affairs, and in a monastic sort of fellowship, with novitiates and initiates, sought to lead an exclusively otherworldly, holy life. These were the Essenes, whose roots also went back to the Assideans of Maccabean times, but whose piety was directed completely inward. They numbered about four thousand and lived on the eastern fringes of the land. Theirs was the life of a primitive commune, with no personal ownership of property or possession. They tilled the soil and cultivated the palm tree, abjured any slave economy and gave expression to their insistence upon ritual cleanliness and religious purity by early morning immersion. They were united with one another in communal and ritual meals, and they carefully nurtured in their midst the ancient heritage of prophetic predictions. They were skilled in the lore of the herbs of the woods, and with them healed the sick. From this fact apparently their name originates, for in Aramaic *assia* is the word for physician. They concerned themselves, too, with the problems of spiritual healing and salvation and with the secrets of the universe as applied to the destiny of the individual. In fact, they were merely religious individualists whose beliefs inevitably led them away from Judaism. From their midst emerged the figure of John the Baptist.

Midway between the extreme worldliness of the Sadducees and the extreme unworldliness of the Essenes stood the Pharisees. It was only they who recognized what was needed at the time, and to the very end they hewed firmly to the line of the Law of God and the People of God, which Ezra had drawn for them in an earlier age.

12

Revolt and End

Such was the spiritual atmosphere of Judea, when the death of Herod set the land aflame. That the tyrant had served his Roman masters well, and was appreciated for it, is amply borne out by the fact that the governing power respected his last will and testament and permitted his kingdom to be divided among his three sons, Antipas, Archilaus and Philip, who were appointed Tetrarchs. But the Tetrarchs were not equal to the crisis confronting them, and it required the mighty power of the Roman legions to squelch the uprising. So it was that shortly after, in the year 6 c.e., Judea was formally annexed to the empire as a province, and was henceforth ruled by Roman Procurators. This only served to add fuel to the fires of revolt, for the constant presence of foreign troops in the land acted as a further, infuriating provocation. Everywhere the Roman eagle was to be seen. On all sides the Roman coinage, with the head of the Emperor graven on it, circulated—on all sides too, the Roman paganism. Added to all this were excessive taxes, encroachments, and force. In this sea of tumult and oppression two trends were apparent among the people. On the one side the visionary Essenes whispered into the ears of the people predictions of salvation through the imminent coming of the Messiah and the establishment of the Kingdom of God on earth. And on the other hand, a new party, known as Zealots, demanded immediate action since for them the Pharisaic policy under such conditions seemed inadequate. Once again, as in the days of Jeremiah, the fever of patriotic action burned high and drew to its ranks the vigorous youth. The Pharisees rendered unto Caesar that which was Caesar's. For them the power they possessed in the Sanhedrin was sufficient. They saw that the Zealots, like the Sadducees, placed fatherland above Law. Their piety, suddenly become political, was suspect in the eyes of the Pharisees and fraught with danger. For them Israel's impregnable fortress was the Divine Law, and as the land went up in flames, they guarded that fortress, patiently waiting their turn.

Augustus Caesar died in the year 14 C.E., and he was succeeded by Tiberius, in whose reign Jesus of Nazareth was crucified by the Romans at the command of the Procurator Pontius Pilate. In the year 37 C.E., Caius Caligula mounted the throne and a new surprise was in store for Judea. The Emperor placed his favorite, the Hasmonean princeling Agrippa, in charge of Judea, and threw in the crown for good measure. Agrippa, dissolute in his youth, charming in maturity, tried to give the land peace, but it was only a short breathing spell. Caligula put the patience of the people to the severest test by demanding for himself homage as for a god. In Alexandria, the anti-Semite Apion carried on his pernicious propaganda. The people rose against Caligula's demands. A terrible wave of persecution broke out, spilling over into Judea, despite the efforts of Agrippa to prevent it. The Jewish philosopher Philo of Alexandria (Philo Judaeus) led a mission to Rome. Agrippa, still in the Emperor's favor, did what he could. But now the Emperor went so far as to demand that his statue be set up in the Temple in

Jerusalem. However his sudden death, in the year 41 C.E., freed Judea from its worries for the time being.

Although Claudius, who ruled from 41 to 54 C.E., confirmed Agrippa in his position and left him his not altogether unimportant kingdom, the fever had by this time gripped the entire people. When Agrippa I died in the year 44 C.E., the Romans did not deem it practical to entrust the full rule to his minor son Agrippa II, and once again the same storm signals appeared as at the termination of Herod's rule. The entire country was in a turmoil. Political desperados and religious fanatics swarmed through the land. The Pharisees were on guard, but their young people stormed out of the schools to join the ranks of the Zealots and guerrillas, or even the ranks of the terroristic "Sicarli," for whom the dagger was the arm of their policy.

Claudius died in the year 54 C.E., and Nero reigned in Rome. Then in the year 64 C.E. there appeared on the scene the last of the Procurators, Gessius Florus, who, unlike his predecessors, consciously tried to drive the drama to its logical conclusion by encouraging anarchy and heaping provocation upon provocation. Revolt was now in full swing, and the Governor Cestius Gallus, rushing in to help, tried in vain to beat down the uprising. It was now too late, and by the year 66 C.E. not a single Roman soldier was left on Judean soil. In the spring of 67, General Flavius Vespasianus appeared with his legions, charged with the task of putting down the turbulence once and for all. The last glorious fight of the people began. The Zealot leaders Simon bar Giora and John of Gischala led the revolt. The defense of Galilee in the north was entrusted to Joseph, who later emerged as the historian, Flavius Josephus. Vespasian advanced slowly. He was compelled to battle every inch of the way. Josephus finally surrendered and went over to the other side. By the beginning of the year 70 C.E., Jerusalem, overflowing with pilgrims from the East and with refugees, was surrounded and besieged. At this juncture Nero died, and Vespasian returned to Rome to assume the imperial crown. His son Titus completed the task. In Jerusalem bloodshed raged. But what inner dissension had failed to achieve, hunger finally won. On the 17th of Tammuz sacrifices in the Temple ceased because of the lack of cattle. The end came on the 9th of Ab in the year 70. Jerusalem had fallen. The Temple was in flames.

While the forces of Vespasian were still besieging Jerusalem, a coffin was carried from the city. It contained the living body of the Pharisaic leader Jochanan ben Zakkai. Once clear of the city he made his way to the Roman general and asked him for permission to set up an academy, with his scholars, in the little village of Jamnia on the Mediterranean coast. Vespasian granted his boon. There in Jamnia, Jochanan waited for the end. When it came, he proclaimed his academy as the official center of Judaism, replacing the Temple site, and with the remnant of the scholars who had escaped the savage Roman fury, he set up a new Sanhedrin.

13

Jesus, Paul and the Church

When this occurred, forty years had already elapsed since Pontius Pilate, the Roman Procurator, had, according to gospel, ordered the crucifixion of Jesus of Nazareth who had carried on his work of preaching and healing throughout Judea. Jesus was the founder of Christianity whose doctrines were destined to sweep over the world, civilizing the barbarians and shaping the course of history for centuries to come. The Gospels represent him as being in fullest opposition to the official Judaism of the Pharisees and Sadducees, as well as to priest and high priest, who in his sight were nothing but exponents of Pharisaism. In that respect he was like the prophets, and yet, at bottom, there was a fundamental difference. The prophets only laid bare the hollow self-contradiction of pious outward concern for religious rites and inward moral depravity, but they kept their feet firmly planted on the soil of the earthly order. Jesus, on the other hand, stood against priest and scribe as the "Son of Man," responsible only to himself and to God. Never before had a religious teacher in Israel given his message with such an emphasis upon the ego and such implications of co-divinity as did he: "Verily I say unto you" was his watchword. That of the prophets had been: "Thus saith the Lord." For this reason, and for this reason alone, Judaism could not accept him and considered him the destroyer of tradition—not only because with an unusual self-assuredness he laid claim to being the Messiah sprung from the house of David, and the "Son of God," but because in his religious doctrine he presented and established the complete isolation and self-responsibility of the individual soul. Judaism's ideal was to strive mightily after the great synthesis between heaven and earth, God and the world, soul and body, spirit and flesh, intent and act, content and form, individual and community. Jesus of Nazareth represented just the opposite, and this he embodied not only in his life and teaching, but also in his suffering and death. "My kingdom is not of this world," he declared, and placed full emphasis upon heaven as against earth, upon spirit as against flesh, upon intent as against act, and in his gospel was fundamentally concerned not with earthly relationships but with his Kingdom of Heaven. Quite consistently he praised a trust in God at the expense of work, a love that goes beyond justice, a transcendent self-denial, and a social order that excludes the wealthy. In those parts of his Sermon on the Mount, which rested squarely on the soil of Judaism—e.g., in the question of charity, prayer and fasting—he shows himself not merely in spirit, but even in words, a true Pharisee. He speaks powerfully, but completely in the spirit of the Scribes, whose best representatives and leaders were indeed wise and pious men. The love of one's enemy which he calls for had long before been proclaimed by the writer of Proverbs: "If thine enemy be hungry, give him bread to eat, and if he be thirsty, give him water to drink" (Proverbs 25:21). Consequently, as a thorough student of the Scriptures Jesus ought not to have said: "Ye have heard that it is written: Thou shalt love thy neighbor and hate thine enemy— but I say unto you. . . ." That he thus expressed himself and not otherwise explains the opposition that he encountered among the people as a religious individualist. In this opposition, we can perhaps find the human and psychological reasons for his own hostility against them.

His work was completed by the Jew, Saul of Tarsus, who took the name Paul, and thirty years later journeyed through the Mediterranean world to preach the gospel of the master whom he himself had never seen. He proclaimed Jesus the Christ-Messiah, and the "fulfiller of the Law." That is to say, he abrogated the Mosaic Law, and in this way it was possible for him to form a new doctrine which would prove acceptable to the Greco-Roman world. It was indeed accepted. He also preached the crucified and resurrected Christ, whose sacrificial death on the cross reconciles with God for all time the truly faithful. And finally he organized, developed and nurtured the first Christian religious communities in the diaspora, and thereby laid the foundations of the Church, which gradually grew out of these primitive Christian communities. With this, laws, cult and order developed anew, but above all something that gave binding unity and stability to the new teaching: Paul created the dogmas, and with the dogmas the defense against any religious individualism.

14

The Triumph of Law

The Pharisees constantly stood midway between the extreme worldliness of the Sadducees and the extreme unworldliness of the Essenes. And in spurning the terrorism of the Zealots who had emerged from their own midst, they showed that they repudiated worldly armaments even as a means to an end. It was their act of founding a school, at the moment of national destruction, that in truth proved the salvation for the nation and assured it a future. Yet in spite of that, their historic achievement lies even deeper. It is to be found in the activity of their schools, the study, teaching and handing-on of Israel's Law, whose study they had cultivated since the time of Ezra.

The belief in the divine inspiration of the Torah demanded an unswerving conviction of its uniqueness, eternity and inexhaustibility. Every word, every phrase had its place. Not a word was superfluous. In their researches the scholars aimed at two things. If there was something that seemed to have been omitted from the Torah, they sought to find it between the lines. And if there was something seemingly superfluous in the lines of the Holy Writ, they sought to explain its presence and interpret it. In this way they were sure to establish the word of God beyond all shadow of doubt. This activity they called *midrash*, that is, study, research or interpretation, and this activity is contained in the very name they gave to their schools—*bet hamidrash* (house of research). However, to preserve the divine perfection of the Torah they permitted it alone to be written down and called it the Written Law. However, they handed on the whole mass of laws stemming from tradition and connected it with the Written Law by the process of interpretation, giving to it the name of Oral Law. This Oral Law was divided into two parts. The most important part, which was an expansion of the legalistic portions of the Law, was known as *halacha* (path, norm) and added to the body of Jewish religious, social and economic jurisprudence. All poetical and narrative portions were termed *agada;* directed as they were to the ethical edification of the people, they belonged more to the synagogue than to the *bet hamidrash.* The time finally came when the mass of material of the Oral Law demanded that the wheat be separated from the chaff, and that the methods of interpretation and deduction be systematized. This is the great contribution of Hillel of Babylonia, who was head of the Sanhedrin *(Nassi)* during the rule of Herod. He set up seven rules or principles of interpretation *(Middot)* which gave system and direction to the new method of research. These rules of Hillel, which were later expanded from seven to thirteen, rested upon the principles of deduction of *halachot* from the text by inference, analogy, reasoning from general to particular and from particular to general. Thus were developed new laws to meet changing conditions, but laws which were firmly rooted in the long line of unbroken tradition, and in this sense could be justly termed *Halacha from Sinai.* The School of Hillel *(Bet Hillel)* became renowned. It had, however, a great and noble rival in the House of Shammai *(Bet Shammai)* led by his contemporary and vice-president *(Av Bet Din)* of the Sanhedrin, the stern Shammai.

When the Temple fell and the visible Jewish state tottered, there was already in existence a powerful unseen realm to sustain the people—the realm of the Torah. Generations of rabbis in their constant application to the study and expansion of the Torah as a living force had reared a mighty structure of the spirit in the body of the oral tradition. This new structure operated as a kind of invisible state for the people, when the visible state structure crumbled. But the Romans paid absolutely no attention to this internal development. It took them a full fifty years more to discover just why they were not done with the Jewish people. Certainly, they had dragged the Jewish leaders to Rome to grace the triumph of Titus and then face execution. They sold the cream of the Jewish youth into the slavery of the Egyptian mines. And yet Israel's Law had shown itself to be far stronger than the Law of the Roman sword.

In the year 116, under the reign of Trajan, the Jews of the Eastern Mediterranean rose in revolt again, and Jewish, Greek and Roman blood flowed in torrents. It lasted for fifteen years until Rome tried to do what it had not yet attempted. Now it attempted to completely destroy the Jews by extirpating their law and religion. All the other emperors, with the exception of the power-maddened Caligula, had carefully avoided interfering with Jewish religion or Jewish law. But in the reign of Hadrian, in the year 130 C.E., a wave of religious persecution, surpassing in intensity that of Antiochus Epiphanes, burst forth. However now it was too late. The rabbis had not rested idly in the fifty years of grace that had been granted them. Not long after the destruction of Jerusalem, the Sanhedrin was headed by Rabban

Gamliel II, a scion of the House of Hillel. With a passion and sternness that many of his own generation misunderstood, he demanded unyielding obedience to his authority and to the Law. Thereby Jewish organized life and leadership both in Judea and the diaspora was so strengthened that the Roman powers arrived at the recognition of the true source of Jewish strength and survival just a little too late. When, in that year, over the ruins of Jerusalem, Hadrian reared the pagan Aelia Capitolina which no Jew could enter, and when he introduced brutally repressive laws which punished with death the observance of Jewish rites or the study of the Torah, he succeeded only in inciting the people to a final despairing revolt—which was rather a terrible war than a revolt—under the leadership of Bar Cochba. But he failed of his principal objective. Simon Bar Cochba, the messianic hero of the Jews, fell in battle at Betar after an heroic struggle that lasted for five years. And with his fall the entire uprising collapsed. But the Rabbinic leaders of the people not only refused to yield, they sealed their historic loyalty to Israel and the Torah with perhaps the most moving martyrdom in all Jewish history. The story of the "Ten Martyrs" is an epic of Jewish heroism and devotion. Rabbi Ḥanina ben Teradyon met his death at the stake, with a Torah scroll wrapped around him. Rabbi Akiba was flayed alive by his tormentors. But Akiba did not die with his work undone. He it was who, traveling around the Mediterranean world, had rallied the people around the banner of Bar Cochba. And more important still, it was he—recognizing the real purpose of the Roman assault—who began to assemble the harvest of the Oral Law. In his school he lifted the ban upon writing down the Oral Law, and, with his pupil Rabbi Meir leading, set them on the course of recording it in writing. We know today that, although in the continued struggles against Rome between 70 and 135 an entire body of literature was lost, the Bible and the Law were rescued. While the generations of the great rabbis sanctified the name of God in death, while Judea, bleeding from a thousand wounds, lost its very name and was forced to call herself Syria-Palestine (Philistina), Rabbi Meir and his comrades sat for sixty years in their schools and did nothing but gather and write down the imperishable material of the Jewish spiritual heritage.

So effective was this work that by the year 200 the last of the great patriarchs of the Sanhedrin, Rabbi Judah Hanassi, known also in Talmudic literature as the "Holy One" or simply "Rabbi," was able to complete the work of the disciples of Rabbi Akiba in Sepphoris. He was the creator of the Mishna (teaching), the first systematically arranged, written version of the Oral Law. It was divided into six major divisions (sedarim): Law of the Fields, Law of Festivals, Law for Women, Civil Law, Temple Law and Law of Ritual Purity and Cleanliness. Each major division was divided into tractates (masechtot), and each tractate is subdivided into sections called perakim. Those traditions which were doubtful versions or of uncertain authority were not included in the Mishna, but were collected nevertheless. They remained "outside" the Mishna, and the Aramaic name given to this collection, Baraitha, means just that. But out of this there grew a new collection, which bore the name Tosefta (Addition). In Jewish law the Baraitha is merely subsidiary. The final collection of the Tosefta was completed in the third century by the pupils of Rabbi Judah Hanassi. These were the first Amoraim (i.e., the Completers) who still lived in Palestine. It is the name given to the teachers of the post-Mishnaic period, who are to be distinguished from the Tannaim, the teachers of the Mishnaic period. Gradually the title Rabbi made way for a new title of Rav, and it is by this means that we distinguish the Tannaim from the Amoraim. The work of the Amoraim was climaxed three centuries later with the creation of the Talmud.

15

The Babylonian Talmud

"Rabbi" died in the year 218 at the ripe old age of eighty. In the compilation of the Mishna, he left behind him for succeeding generations the rich legacy of a new code of laws that took its place beside the Torah (Pentateuch) and was accepted as binding by world Judaism. Like the Five Books of Moses in earlier times, it now became the predominant object of constant study, research and exposition. The completion of the Mishna, in effect, marked the end of the spiritual history of Palestine for the time being. The center of Jewish creativity began to shift. To be sure, the institution of the Patriarchate survived "Rabbi" by some two centuries. To be sure his disciples Rav Jochanan and Resh Lakish carried on in Tiberias. Nevertheless the culmination of the Mishna was the last, albeit magnificent gasp of a Judea in its death agony. The long line of descendants of the House of Hillel that occupied the Patriarchate for four centuries came to an end with the death of the childless Gamaliel VI. Later, after many years of shadowy existence, the portals of the Sanhedrin swung shut (c. 425 C.E.).

The star of Babylonia was in the meantime rising again. In the third century Ardeshir I founded the Empire of the Sassanids. He revived the ancient religion of Zoroaster (Zarathustra), and on the base of this faith in the god of light, Ahuramazda, he founded a Persian state, which for three centuries stood out as a powerful and independent rival of Roman might, and was to become a new great center in the onward march of Judaism and of the Jewish people. It was indeed a significant portent of the shape of things to come when Aba Areka, known in the Talmud as Rav, and Mar Samuel, usually referred to more briefly as Samuel, two eminent disciples of Judah Ha-nassi, left Palestine for Babylonia soon after the death of their master, there to set up two academies. Rav went to Sura, on the Euphrates, and Samuel to Nehardea. When, in the year 260, Nehardea became the battleground of conflicting armies and was destroyed, its place was taken by the Academy at Pumbeditha, which was founded by the teachers Raba and Abaye. These were jurists of the highest caliber, and under their guidance their academy rose to fame and distinction. In these academies the Mishna formed the basis of further study and research, and it remained thus for the next three centuries.

In Palestine, both temporal and spiritual authority had been united in the office of Patriarch. In Babylonia, however, there was a distinction between the head of the academy and the so-called Exilarch (*Rosh Gola, Resh Galuta*). The Exilarch, who laid claim to descent from the House of David, was recognized by the state as the titular head of the Jewish people of the realm during the period of the Sassanids, and later during that of the Arab Caliphs. He had in effect the status of a temporal prince. He maintained a magnificent court in the capital, and exercised the authority of an almost supreme administrative official. The academy head was the leading religious authority, and besides was usually a sort of chief justice. In harmony and cooperation, temporal and spiritual authority worked together for many centuries to lead the Babylonian Jewish community to a great period of blossoming and efflorescence. But later on, around the year 950, the general confusions of the era are reflected in bitter conflicts between the two offices.

The great achievement of the Babylonian Jewish community of that time was the Talmud. Twice each year, before Passover and New Year, for the entire months of Adar and Elul (these two months are known as the Kalla—the Months of Assembly) the scholars of the Academies would gather under the leadership of the academy head to carry on lengthy discussions and disputations on problems arising out of the Mishna. Passage by passage would be considered, probed and illuminated by living examples, and concluded by definite decisions. Then as the festival approached, the academy head would come to the synagogue and for an entire week devote himself to the task of interpreting in simple and popular fashion the principles of Jewish law to the common people. In this way, a living bridge was fashioned between doctrine and people.

This process of development went smoothly forward until, toward the end of the fourth century, the currents of uncertainty for the Jews in the realm of the Sassanids began to quicken again. But the Academy of Sura had the good fortune to produce, in the person of Rav Ashi, a man who was fully equal to the challenges of the time. For sixty years he guided the destinies of the Academy and devoted his entire life to bringing together the mountainous mass of new developments in the exposition and application of the Jewish law and preparing this body of material for ultimate codification. In this work he made particularly effective use of the "Kalla" months. During this period he had the scholars apply themselves with especial care to the task of going through the Mishna sentence by sentence in order to cast the many deductions in clear-cut, pithy statements. This work lasted for thirty years, and then another revision was undertaken. It was left to his disciple Ravina, however, in collaboration with Rav Jose, head of the Academy of Pumbeditha, to bring the work to its conclusion. The result of this mammoth effort was the Talmud—that is to say, the text of the Mishna plus the product of centuries of elaboration and expansion in the academies which was known as the Gemara (completion). In its more specific title it is known as the Talmud Bavli or Babylonian Talmud. A similar development, begun in Palestine in the third century, brought forth the so-called Talmud Yerushalmi, the Palestinian Talmud. This remained incomplete and—codified about the year 370—did not gain legal sanction within the Jewish people.

Rav Ashi had a strong premonition of the future and he was not, indeed, wrong. For fifty years after his death the Sassanids undertook to apply the Hadrianic pattern to Babylonian Jewish life, and a wave of intense persecution was unleashed. The study of the Torah was outlawed, and synagogues and academies were destroyed. But the Talmud had already been compiled. The Gemara was completely codified and arranged. To be sure, the next generation of teachers and scholars, known as Saboreans ("annotators"), continued working away whipping the whole structure into final shape, but the bulk of the work had been achieved. Once again the way of religious persecution had come just a little too late to be effective in destroying this structure. Judaism had taken a great stride forward in its spiritual and physical development and was well able to weather the storm. The final codification of the Talmud was completed in the middle of the sixth century.

It is an utter impossibility to give a brief synopsis of the contents of the Talmud. Apt indeed is the traditional reference to it as a veritable "sea." This "sea of the Talmud" is an accurate, composite mirror of the inner and outer life of the Jewish people for a period that spans a thousand years. Its contents are not confined to religious law. Indeed, it gives a comprehensive picture of the religious, ethical, philosophic, scientific, educational and popular, in a word, the entire cultural history of the people. This book of a thousand years contains everything pertaining to home and hearth, custom and usage, history and myth, simile and proverb, life and learning, thinking and feeling, faith and even superstition. It is indeed an encyclopedia with a thousand contributors, for such indeed were the long line of rabbis. This accounts for the varying and oft-times even contradictory points of view that one is likely to encounter in its pages. The style of the Talmud is all its own, brief and pithy to the point of being cryptic. It defies effective translation. Even the original text would be almost impossible to understand were it not for the famous commentary of Rashi (1040–1105). It was Rashi who first was able to solve and explain the peculiar formulations of the Talmud, its difficult style and its lack of punctuation, by a simple common sense interpretation of the text. His was the key that opened wide to later generations the gateway to an intelligent understanding of the Talmud. It became necessary to read in full the text of Rashi (which was more extensive by far than the text of the Talmud itself), to understand the latter.

A book such as this, that was a thousand years in the making, and that was sired by a thousand authors, cannot be judged by the consideration of details here and there. One must attempt to look upon it as a whole. As an entity the Talmud is not merely a vast encyclopedia of Jewish knowledge and Jewish life. It is very much more than that. It is a book whose every line is sanctified with the spirit of holiness. Its laws are overflowing with the ideal of justice and love of mankind. In them lives the spirit of Moses. In them the spirit of the prophets finds a magnificent expression in the sublime delicacy of their religious morality. The few lines here cited, picked from the Talmud at random, serve to lift a corner of the veil and to give a fleeting insight into the brilliant light of Talmudic morality. Here is what the Talmud has to say concerning the three fundamental functions of Jewish religiosity—Prayer, Penitence and Love:

"What is worship of the heart? *Prayer.*—Let your words before the Holy One, praised be He, ever be brief.—Know before whom you stand!—Let every man cleanse his heart of sin before he begins to pray.—To cry over spilt milk is a false prayer.—Here you have a short prayer: 'Thy will be done in heaven above. Grant joyfulness of heart them that fear Thee here on earth, and do what seemeth good in Thine own eyes! Praised be Thou, O Lord, that hearest prayer!'"

"Those who have done *penance* have more merit than those who have never sinned.—Let a man always consider himself half innocent and half guilty. Happy is he who does a good deed! By so doing he tilts the scale in the favor of his merit. Woe to him who commits a sin. He tilts the scale in the direction of his guilt.—It is not sack-cloth and fasting that bring about forgiveness, but rather making amends and good deeds."

"*Love of humanity* is more than charity.—The value of charity lies only in love, which lives in it.—Love surpasses charity in three respects: Charity touches only a man's money; love touches the man himself. Charity is only for the poor; love is for both poor and rich. Charity is only for the living; love is for the both living and dead.—Love without reproof of error is no love.—He who judges his neighbor leniently will himself be judged leniently by God. Let man always be intelligent and affable in his God-fearing. Let him answer softly, curb his wrath and let him live in peace with his brethren and his kin and with every man, yes, even with the pagan on the street, in order that he be beloved in heaven and on earth, and be acceptable to all men.— The kindly man is the truly God-fearing man."

16

Rome's Decline and Persia's Fall

While the Jews were thus occupied in their houses of study delving into the Law of God, and building that "fence about the Torah" that was to protect Israel from the ravages of paganism and barbarianism, that Empire which had wrought the ruin of Jerusalem was itself visited with decline and destruction. The Roman Emperors became military dictators who were compelled to hurl their legions from one end of the Empire to the other in order to maintain their conquests, and they finally found it an utter impossibility to keep it together. It began to crumble in the east—we saw the first signs of this in the rise of the Sassanids in Persia—and Rome was too far off in the west to be able to enforce its rule effectively. The Emperor Constantine (323–337) founded Byzantium-Constantinople and made it his imperial seat. On his deathbed he went over to Christianity and in this way appeared to have saved the Empire again. In the alternating game of the persecution and tolerance played by the various Emperors, this new faith had grown tremendously in strength and influence. In its early stages it had adapted itself to Greek thought. Paul the Apostle made his contributions, which were intended to sunder the new faith from its parent Judaism and to graft the new teaching successfully upon the tree of Greco-Latin civilization. By this dual process Christianity made enormous headway in the Greco-Roman world. Such compromises the leaders of Rabbinic Judaism, because of their beliefs, could not and would not make. In the midst of the mounting confusion of the world, Christianity won countless adherents and penetrated every corner of Roman officialdom. It became the state religion, and in turn began to apply the principle of intolerance, from which it had suffered so, to those faiths that differed from it. Its newly-won, youthful power seemed to exclude tolerance. With the transfer of the Sabbath day from Saturday to Sunday (around the year 310) the rift with Judaism was made complete.

Despite this, the Roman Empire as a temporal state was beyond rescue. The barbarians first split it asunder and then destroyed it completely. From Hungary swooped the Vandals; from Rumania the Visigoths. Behind them swarmed the Ostrogoths from Russia, and on the steppes of Asia the Huns stood poised. The Vandals pierced the Danube barrier and there was no holding them anymore. Between 400 and 450 the barbarian hordes inundated the Roman Empire. In the year 410 Alaric took Rome. The Vandals in the meantime drove through Spain to North Africa, set up a pirate state on the site of Carthage and plundered the entire Mediterranean area. In the meantime, in the Far East the Huns were set into motion. Like a swarm of locusts they swept through Europe, destroying all before them. Their ruler Attila (424) gained mastery from Asia to the Rhine, and the flood-tide of his conquests was only checked in bloody battle on the Catalonian fields to the south of France. In 475 the Vandals conquered Rome and were able to send the tidings to Byzantium that no Roman Emperor ruled there any more. Rome had fallen, but the Church survived. The Bishop of Rome assumed the rule over the Latin world, and began, as Pope, to rule the Christian world.

The Byzantine-Greek half of the Roman Empire was better able to withstand the tidal wave of the Hun and Vandal onslaught. Indeed it even experienced a flourishing period in the sixth century under the rule of the energetic Emperor Justinian (527–565). Just about the same time when the Babylonian Talmud was receiving its final form, he completed the codification of the Roman Law, the great achievement of his lifetime. In this code of law, he included a series of edicts concerning the Jews which contained all the limitations and restrictions that had grown up in the two centuries since Christianity had risen to power as state religion. This legislation completely excluded Jews from holding public office and reduced them to the status of second class citizenship.

But the Jews had once again completed their work. By the time the Empire of the Sassanids, in whose boundaries they had found a century of uncertain protection, was locked in its death struggle with Byzantium at the beginning of the seventh century, the gigantic creation of the Talmud, the codification of more than ten centuries of development in Jewish life, had been completed. The tempest of the barbarians had shaken the world, but it did not touch this Jewish achievement. The Jews suffered the torments of persecution on all sides, in Byzantium and in Persia, by Christians and Magii. Their autonomy was shattered, their exilarchs beheaded, their children forcibly converted, their Sabbath prohibited. But their enemies, who were at one another's throats at the same time, did not, meanwhile, have time to perceive that a new storm was gathering in the deserts of Arabia which would sweep over the world and bring in its wake a new breathing spell of freedom for the Jews. Around the year 630 the Emperor and the Sassanid received from a certain Mohammed twin messages with the same content: "Surrender!"

17

The Jews of Bagdad

Mohammed of Mecca created a new religion by combining the elements of Arabic folk religion with Judaism and Christianity. Islam has indeed, with much truth, been called "Judaism covered with the sand of the desert." From Judaism, which he came to know through his journeys in Arabia and Syria, Mohammed borrowed the idea of pure monotheism, and to it he added as the five pillars of his faith: confession, prayer, fasting, alms, and the pilgrimage. He called the faith Islam, i.e., complete surrender to the will of God. In that concept lay the strong fatalism of predestination ("Allah knows it!" "Allah wills it!") which gave to Islam its aggressive power and enthusiasm. At first Mohammed made a strong effort to win over the numerous Judeo-Arabic tribes round about him to his new faith. Failing in this he became their bitter opponent and subsequently rooted them out almost completely. But he did succeed in uniting all the Arab tribes under the banner of his new faith and launching them upon a career of world conquest, whose beginnings he himself lived to see, and whose brilliance, extent and swiftness is to be compared only with the meteoric rise of Alexander the Great. Now the East, in the form of Islam, was able to repay the West with interest for its gift of the ten preceding centuries, Hellenism. Beginning though it did with primitive religious concepts, Islam blossomed forth in a relatively short time into a world civilization of brilliant stature.

Islam gained its world conquest with an unbelievable rapidity. Eight years after the death of Mohammed in 632 it already held Jerusalem, Damascus and Mesopotamia. For a second time Judaism witnessed the decline of a Persian Empire. At the same time the Bedouins spilled over into Egypt and North Africa. Spain was invaded in the year 710, and ten years later the bearers of Islam stood at the peaks of the Pyrenees. It was only at the Battle of Poitiers, in 732, that the onslaught was checked by the united Frankish tribes under Charles Martel and a western boundary was set up against the Arabic torrent at the Pyrenees.

Two factors made this conquest significant and fruitful: the meeting with the ancient cultures and the successful mixture of races on the soil of Spain. Out of a fusion of the aboriginal stock with the stream of migration from North Africa there emerged the creative, talented Andalusians. There also, as in Persia, the Bedouins encountered the learning of the Jews which awakened them to fruitful endeavor. In Egypt they came in contact with the heritage of Greece, and at once there blossomed among a people that had just emerged from the desert a culture and civilization which far outstripped the older Latin-ecclesiastical order of the Mediterranean world. Mathematics, medicine, physics and astronomy came back to Europe with the Arabs. To this day, many of these sciences owe much of their terminology to the Arabic tongue of that day. They were founders, above all else, of the science of philology and grammar. No people, from beggar to prince, so loved and cultivated its native tongue with quite the passion that the Arabs did. Side by side with the sciences, poetry and architecture began to flourish. The art of poetry indeed became a common possession of the entire people. This great culture that had shot up with the breathtaking rapidity of a century of achievement rested, by the year 900, upon the two mighty pillars of Bagdad and Cordova, in the East and West. These two great cities, the centers of the great academies of the Orient and Occident, were indeed the massive supports that upheld the spiritual arch of the great Islamic civilization.

Wherever the Arabs came as conquerors, they were greeted by the Jews as redeemers and emancipators. Despite the fact that Mohammed's dislike for Jews cropped up among his successors, despite the fact that the first Caliphs introduced some laws of discrimination against the Jews, despite the fact that there was an occasional outburst of violence as an outgrowth of religious fanaticism—despite all this, it must be clearly borne in mind that for Judaism as a whole the contact with Islam was as fruitful and enriching as had been the contact with Hellenism. Perhaps even more so, for between Arab and Jew were common roots that ran deep—a common racial ancestry, a common ancestry of speech, and a deep understanding of one another's thought and research processes. This all resulted in a development and enrichment which both cultures enjoyed mutually, both gaining immensely from the contact with each other. Such an interaction between two cultures and two religions had never before, and perhaps has never since, occurred with such mutually enriching results.

When the Arabs came to Bagdad, the center of the Orient, Judaism blossomed forth once more as though touched with a magic wand. It was not long before Jews were speaking and writing Arabic as their vernacular. There began the great period of the Gaonim (650–1040).

The autonomy of the Jews grew in strength and effectiveness. The exilarch acquired greater power and prestige than ever. The academies received a new lease on life. The academy heads, the Gaonim (Gaon-Excellency), acquired a widespread influence such as they had never before enjoyed. Their famous decisions on questions of Jewish Law (Responsa), which came to them from every corner of the diaspora, testify to the extent of their authority.

This authority was strong enough to weather even an attempted schism in Jewish life that cropped up in Bagdad in the eighth century. This was the anti-rabbinic sect of the Karaites. This movement must be understood against the background of the intense currents of religious activity and development in Babylonian Judaism after the decline of the Sassanids and the rise of Islam. Mysticism and skepticism, authority and freedom of thought, were seething in the minds of all people of thought. A certain Anan ben David succeeded in bringing together the many forces of the opposition and uniting them within the folds of the sect known as Karaites or B'nai Mikra (i.e., Exclusive Supporters of the Biblical Text). They rejected the body of Oral Law as embodied in the Talmud, and accepted only the authority of the Bible in its strict literal interpretation. During the following centuries, as a result of their careful studies and researches into the Bible, the Karaites reached a high degree of spiritual and literary achievement which was heightened, too, by the vigorous opposition of the Rabbanites, those who remained faithful to the Rabbinic tradition. But their reversion to the strict literal Biblical text rendered life much harder for them and acted as an oppressive, restraining force upon their followers. For that reason the sect never grew to any considerable proportions. Remnants of it are to this day to be found in the Crimea, in the Balkans and in Egypt. Its development and passing period of efflorescence within the Babylonian Talmudic world are testimony to the extent of the religious freedom that prevailed under Arab rule.

The age of the Gaonim reached its peak in the personality of the great Gaon Saadya (892–942). Saadya was born in Fayyum, Egypt, and was called to the Academy of Sura in 933 as its head. He was the first eminent Jewish scholar to write in Arabic, and it was he who translated the Bible into that tongue. He was also the author of many significant works in both Arabic and Hebrew. This was the outstanding period of splendor for the great Arab Academies of Bagdad and Basra and the great school of religious philosophy known as the Kalam. Schooled in the philosophies of Aristotle and the Neo-Platonists, which had by this time been translated into the Arabic, this school set out to reconcile reason with revelation. Proof of the existence of God, freedom of will and providence were the major problems with which Arab rationalism grappled. Equipping himself from the rich intellectual arsenal of the Arabic schools, Saadya was the first Jew to present a systematic, philosophic presentation of Judaism. This he did in a monumental book which he wrote in Arabic, and which bears the name of "The Problems of Faith and Knowledge" (Hebr. *Emunot v'De'ot*). In it he set forth his faith, defended it against the opposing views of the various systems, and became the creator of systematized Jewish religious philosophy. Saadya symbolized the climax of that epoch which to the eleventh century made significant contributions to Jewish life in the development of Jewish liturgy, philology and grammar. But its influence was finally forced to yield to a new and pulsating center that was growing in the West. With the blossoming of the Moorish civilization in Spain, the Jewish communities of the West began to come to the forefront, and by the middle of the tenth century the Spanish Jewish world could already be termed the heart of world Judaism.

18

The Jews of Cordova

Andalusia, the southern part of Spain that extends as far as the River Tajo, was divided into a number of emirates, each bearing the name of its capital city. The most important of these small principalities was Cordova, where, around the year 950, Abdulrahman III ruled in a majesty and splendor that rivalled the Caliphate of Bagdad. He built the stately mosque with its veritable forest of 1,300 massive pillars, and the famous old bridge that spans the Guadalquivir. In his court the arts and sciences flourished under his beneficent encouragement. They flourished, too, in other principalities, in Seville, Malaga and Granada—all of them vying with each other for the laurel of freedom of thought and life. The enchanting dream of the Thousand and One Nights was dreamed here in the West too, and lasted for the better part of five centuries until it began to crumble from a double blow within and without—the influx of the fanatical Almohades coming over from North Africa and the gradual, inexorable march forward of Christian Spain from the north. The last act in this melancholy drama of decline was the fall of Granada in 1492, the last bulwark of Moorish power in Spain, which coincided with the expulsion of the Jews.

The Andalusian epoch is co-extensive with what we call the Golden Age of the Jews in Spain. At the court of Abdulrahman, the leading councillor and diplomatic agent was the Jew Ḥasdai ibn Shaprut. He was a great patron of Jewish learning and a protector of his people. With him we see the beginning of that epoch in which the Jew with political influence took over leadership among the Jewish people. But even though Ḥasdai placed the full weight of his power and prestige behind the advancement of Jewish learning, the fact remains that in the tenth century Spanish Jewry was still outstanding primarily for its external splendor and visible power. Gradually, however, the Hebrew language began to bestir itself with a new vigor. Hebrew poetry began to flourish. Above all, the great academy of Cordova, under the brilliant leadership of Moses ben Ḥanoch, grew in authority and prestige and presently it replaced the Babylonian academies as the effective center of Jewish learning and authority. With the passing of the last of the Gaonim, Sherira and Hai, the reins of leadership slipped from the fingers of Babylonian Jewry and passed on to Spain. Ḥasdai took an active and vital interest in every aspect of Jewish life, and this interest went far afield from his native Cordova, extending to Germany, to Constantinople, yes, even as far as the Caspian Sea. Here he came in contact by correspondence with the Khazars, a Finnish-Ural tribe living on the banks of the Volga, the dim tidings of whose conversion to Judaism two centuries before had penetrated to the West.

In all the courts of Andalusia there now came forward Jews who played leading roles in state affairs. The most famous of these was Samuel ibn Nagrela (Samuel haNagid, or Samuel the Prince). Samuel rose from humble origins to the eminence and authority of Vizier of Granada about the year 1050. The result was that, quite parallel to the upswing of Islamic culture there was an explosive growth of a new Jewish literature.

Most of it was written in Arabic, but all of it was devoted to the development of Judaism, to the study of the Bible, Grammar, and Philosophy. The studies of the Talmud were concentrated and systematized. The Pyrenees were not high enough to hold back this intense flurry of intellectual activities, and their influence was felt with tremendously enriching results in the Jewish communities of Southern France. Indeed these communities became the natural bridge over which these cultural gains passed to the Jewish communities of the remainder of France, of Germany, and to the Christian world as well. In Provence, to the thirteenth century, dwelt the famous families of Kimḥi and Tibbon, natives of Spain, who produced several generations of eminent translators. It was they who translated the great Arabic Jewish classics into Hebrew and made them the heritage of Jews of all lands and all climes. During the selfsame period, the monks of Castile were engaged in translating the great classics of the Arabic world into Latin. Of these, the most eminent philosophic works were the great volumes by the Andalusian, Ibn Rashid (c. 1150) and the Persian, Ibn Sina (c. 1000), who are known as Averroes and Avicenna in the scholastic philosophy of the Church of the Middle Ages. Their influence upon the thought of medieval Europe was truly incalculable.

The achievements of Spanish Jewry reached their apex in the brilliant triple constellation that flashed across the skies of that era of Jewish history that spanned a period of two centuries. These three, Solomon ibn Gabirol, Judah Halevy and Moses ben Maimon (Maimonides), became indeed three great fixed stars on the horizon of Israel's eternity. None of these three had any personal contact with each other. Each was born either shortly before or soon after the death of the other, yet together they form an unbroken chain. Under the skillful hand of the ill-starred, consumption-wracked Gabirol (1020–1070) David's harp came alive and began to sing again in its ancient glory. He sang to God of his aspirations and suffering, in majestic, vibrant Hebrew. As a Jewish neo-Platonist, he wrote a great philosophic work "M'kor Chayim" ("The Fountain of Life") in which he glorified all creation and moral striving as an eternal struggle between form and matter. The book was translated into the Latin by churchmen under the title of *Fons Vitae,* and he was known among the medieval scholastics as Avicebron. This work enriched the thought of medieval Christianity, especially of the Franciscans, and it has only recently been discovered that scholastic Avicebron and the Jew Ibn Gabirol were one and the same person.

The torch of his poetic creativity was passed on to Judah Halevy (1080–1140), who is more famous than Gabirol because of the expression of Israel's undying longing for Zion that is found in his poetry, and because of the dramatic pilgrimage to Palestine that marked the end of his days. He is Gabirol's equal as poet, but not quite his equal in depth and profundity. His Arabic book, the "Kusari," which he cast in the form of a dialogue between the king of Khazars and a rabbi, is more a presentation of an enthusiastic acceptance of an inspired, revealed Judaism than it is a work of systematic philosophy. It was the poet Halevy, not the philosopher, who wrote the book whose sole arguments lie in its mystic deliverance and passion. But that made it the most intimate testament of his life. When it was finished he could not but act on the conclusions of a work in which he had poured forth his soul. He left Spain for his pilgrimage to Palestine. He arrived in Egypt but after that nothing was heard of him again. Nobody knows whether he ever reached the object of his longings or not.

Towering above all else in the next century of Jewish history is the figure of Moses Maimon or Maimuni (Maimonides) (1135–1204). He was born in Cordova and climaxed his career in Cairo as a renowned physician and rabbi. Both in the East and in the West he ruled and influenced Judaism with as much clarifying as revolutionizing power far beyond the temporal span of his days on earth. He was the creator of the first great systematic representation of Talmudic law, the Mishne Torah. Many previous attempts had been made at such compendia, notably among these the effort of Isaac Alfassi (known as the "Rif") who died in Lucena, Spain, in 1104. But Maimonides' effort crowned them all. A Jewish Averroes, persecuted like him and after his death even charged with heresy, he developed in his great philosophic work the *More Nebuchim Guide to the Perplexed*, a philosophic presentation of Judaism on the basis of a strict rationalism. By making reason the measuring rod even of Tradition and Revelation, he frightened the faithful ones, who had been under his strong influence as long as he lived. But when he died the Jewish world was torn asunder. Maimunist and anti-Maimunist hurled bans of excommunication at one another. The grave of the great man was desecrated in Tiberias. His works were denounced, even before the Church authorities, as heretical, and his writings were ordered burnt by the Inquisition of Montpellier. The entire thirteenth century was consumed with struggles centering around the writings of this man, and the Church took part in the fight. In truth, the influence of Maimonides extended right through into modern times.

If we call Spinoza the Father of European "Enlighten-ment," then surely Maimonides was its grandfather. With Maimonides, rationalism stopped short of step-ping outside the bounds of religion and Judaism. Spi-noza took just that step, and the rabbis of Amsterdam who excommunicated him in the year 1656 knew exactly what they were doing, as indeed did the rabbis of four centuries before when, fearful of the conse-quences of its effects upon immature minds, they for-bade the study of the *Guide to the Perplexed* to anyone under the age of twenty-five.

19

Popes and Princes

When Maimonides breathed his last in Cairo in the year 1204, the German monarch Frederick II, the last of the Hohenstaufens, still a child, sat upon the throne of Sicily. He received his education at Palermo. This court was a haven of free thought and free exchange of ideas, where Jew and Arab had unhampered entry, and where Islamic learning was more highly esteemed than the teachings of the Church. In the mind of this ruler, born centuries ahead of his time—and therefore ill-starred and misunderstood—two cultures, the Arabic-Jewish and the Occidental-Christian, met for the first and only time. But his spirit, attacked and persecuted by the Church's ban, was broken.

While the Orient, in those days of Arab glory, scattered its seeds over the lands of the Mediterranean and illuminated the world with the torch of its learning, the northern lands of Europe lived in disorder, disunity and constant wars. This condition was hardly mitigated by the new Feudal System which was gradually evolving. When Charles Martel defeated the Arabs at Poitiers in 732, it was the first time that a strong man appeared in the chaotic North. His son Pippin assumed the rank of king, but it fell to his grandson Charlemagne to add Italy to his Frankish Empire, and to have himself crowned by the Pope in Rome as Holy Roman Emperor in the year 800. It was a dubious gift that Gregory granted the great

Charles. For him, it was the crowning of a world-spanning power. But soon after the death of his son, Louis the Pious, the Empire of Charlemagne began to crumble. France fell in the year 987 to Hugh Capet, and now began a struggle that paralyzed the northern peoples for centuries. Prince stood against Prince, Emperor against Pope. Alongside of this, rivalry flared between the Greek and Roman wings of the Christian Church, climaxing in a final break in the year 1054. The power of the Popes grew. The Emperor Henry had to stand barefoot in the yard of the Papal Castle of Canossa. In Germany, in the meantime, rival Princes struggled for power, while the warlike Normans wrested the control of England from the hands of the Saxons. In this world, torn by strife, the Papacy in greatest need turned to preaching the Crusades to forge unity once again in Christendom through a common aim. The extent of its success in achieving such temporary unity speaks for the influence which Christianity and the Papacy then had.

It was during these times that the Jews experienced the greatest agonies. The space of five centuries had transformed them from Roman citizens to the status of despised pariahs. In the year 612, the Spanish kingdom of the West Goths offered them the choice between baptism and exile. In this hour the first Marranos were born. In France, at the same time, similar tendencies came to the fore. The proselytizing zeal of the church did not flag. In Germany, where Jewish communal life can be traced back by contemporary documents as far as the year 321 (in Cologne), they were placed outside the pale of German Law from the time of Charlemagne onward. Out of letters of protection and permits for settlement, originally issued to individuals, there gradually grew privileges for communities. All these special rights were purchased, and had to be repurchased time and time again. In spite of that Jewish life developed. They were permitted to carry on trade and commerce, they were allowed to own land and property. They enjoyed a period of distinct prosperity. This was cut short sharply by the First Crusade (1096), and as a result of the ensuing disorders Jews acquired the status of Servi Camerae (servants of the royal chamber), a status which from then on was to define the course of Jewish social life. The Jews were considered to be the personal property of the imperial household. In the first stages of those turbulent times, this was a sort of protection. But as the power of the Holy Roman Emperors began to wane and royal finances became low, the Emperors would pawn or sell their "servants of the chamber" or otherwise squeeze every bit of personal advantage out of them that they possibly could.

On top of this came the developments in Canon Law which contributed much more to the humiliation of the Jews than did any law of the state. In this respect the thirteenth century is a gloomy century for the Jews, mitigated only by the issuance of the Papal Bull of Innocent IV (1247) declaring the blood libel to be a falsehood. Otherwise it presented a gloomy picture indeed. At the Fourth Lateran Council of the year 1215, under the leadership of Pope Innocent III, it was decreed that Jews wear the yellow badge. Soon after all intercourse between Christian and Jew was prohibited. The Ghetto came into being. Gregory IX (1227–1241), who carried on the struggle against the hapless Frederick II, arraigned the Jewish books before the Inquisition. He it was who first forbade disputations on religious themes with Jews but finally turned about and ordered them. He it was who instituted the edict compelling Jews to listen to conversion sermons. The Dominicans and Franciscans made this one of their dedicated tasks, and the two centuries between the thirteenth and fifteenth are replete with such compulsory sermons and disputations. The best known of these is the notorious disputation of Tortosa, which went through sixty-five sessions, and lasted almost a full year (1413–14). To loss of civil and political rights was added moral and social degradation, and this latter was a direct result of official Church policy. Hand in hand with these factors during these centuries went the steady elimination of the Jews from the normal economic life. Originally they were active in every field of endeavor, in agriculture, handicrafts, commerce and trade. Now they were gradually excluded from handicrafts by the guilds, and from trade and commerce by the cities. All that was left to them was the huckster's sack and money lending. They did not voluntarily turn to these occupations. They were forced into it. For it was a useful thing for the kings and princes to have at hand ready and helpless victims for plundering when the need for money arose.

During this long period of suffering there were two years in Germany that marked a sort of crest of Jewish agony. They were 1096, the year of the First Crusade, and 1348, the year of the Black Death. One might be tempted to add to these the years 1298 and 1336 as third and fourth crests respectively. In the former year the infamous Rindfleisch, spurred by the false charges of profanation of the host, scourged Swabia with his murderous hordes, wreaking destruction upon one hundred and forty-six communities. In the latter year Armleder and his cohorts swept from the Rhine district to Steiermark, smashing one hundred and twenty communities. But the Crusade and the Black Death, both in their extent and consequences, stand out in such horrible uniqueness that they must perforce be counted milestones in the *via dolorosa* of the Jews of Germany. The first Crusade, preached in order to unite a Europe that was torn by war and strife around one great religious goal, at one stroke destroyed the blossoming Jewish communities of the Upper and Lower Rhineland. Thousands were slain in Treves, Worms, Mainz and Cologne. And when, three centuries later, Europe was ravaged by a dread plague, the infamous charge spread like wildfire that the Jews, by poisoning the wells, were responsible for the catastrophe. Three hundred and fifty communities were plundered and ravaged by the frenzied mob. The agony lasted for three years (1348–1351). Then it was that Poland opened wide her doors to the harried Jews of Germany. The great centers of Jewish settlement in Eastern Europe began to take shape, where to this day are preserved the ancient German garb, in the form of the caftan, and the ancient German tongue, in the form of Yiddish.

But German Jewry was shattered and for a long time to come was unable to lift its head. Even though their development did not reach the peaks of Spanish Jewry, names like Rabbenu Gershom and Rashi, as well as the Tossafists, testify to the vigor of the Jewish spirit in Germany despite suffering and persecution. Rabbenu Gershom (960–1040) lived in Metz. He was one of the fathers of Talmudic learning in Germany and was known as the Light of the Exile (Me'or ha Golah). He it was who issued the famous reform (tekana) putting an end to polygamy among the Jews of Europe. Rashi (1040–1105), the most famous of all Bible and Talmud commentators, was born in southern France, studied at Worms, and carried on his creative work in the city of

Troyes in Lorraine. His followers (the Tossafists), who continued and expanded his great work, proved despite all sufferings that the Jewish spirit was still alive. But the impact of the persecutions following the Black Death was too much in their cumulative effect, and German Jewry began to lapse into an intellectual lethargy. The religious liturgy of the time sang of the tragedies and sufferings in an obscure and difficult speech. Mysticism took hold upon the people. The Kabbala found a fertile soil in their tortured hearts. The Kabbalistic book known as the Zohar, which gained currency around that time, was widely studied and succeeded in confusing many a spirit. The blood-letting had been too great. It seemed as though German Jewry was undergoing its death agonies.

20

Exile from Spain

While the Jews in Germany were suffering from the internal chaos of the land and the declining imperial power which made them the hapless footballs of princely and burgher whims, the early centralization and consolidation of royal power in France and England rendered their situation a good deal different, but no less grave. In France, in the space of two centuries, between 1181 and 1394, they were expelled four times and taken back thrice. Each expulsion was aimed directly at the confiscation of their property, whose liquidation often took years to consummate. And every time they were permitted to return, a healthy contribution to the royal exechequer was involved. In the final expulsion of 1394, 100,000 Jews were compelled to leave the land. In England where Jews had been living even before the eleventh century, they were the personal property of the king, a relationship similar to the status of the "servants of the chamber" in Germany. The kings used them as a sponge. First they would allow them a period of security, then they would squeeze them dry of their possessions. Then another period of quiet followed by another flurry of oppression and robbery. Thus they eked out a tortured existence until the year 1290, when they were expelled from England.

While the story of the Jews in Germany, France and England was being written in blood and tears, Spanish

Jewry continued to bask in the sunlight of continuing prosperity. But here too decline and tragedy lurked just beyond the horizon. And it struck at a time when the outer splendor and civil rights of the Spanish Jews had reached a stage unmatched in almost any other land during the period of the diaspora. They had become assimilated, felt themselves to be Spaniards, and clung passionately to the land of their birth, when the blow fell. This blow was intimately linked up with the general development of the land. The war against the Moors that lasted for four centuries was the dominating factor in the collective mind of Christian Spain and set the direction of the policies of its kings. The inexorable, ruthless drive of the Christian North on the Moslem South rendered Andalusia progressively weaker and acted as a catalyst in spurring the consolidation of the North. By the fourteenth century it was already only a matter of time until the destruction of the Moors and the unification of the Christian North would be completed. The issues were at once national and religious, and the war against Granada both for the kings of Castile and for the Pope in Rome was in reality another Crusade.

The position of the Jews in Castile a century and a half before the expulsion was still an extremely favorable one. In this feudal land, where the insolent nobility and their hidalgo followers lived in fortified castles, keeping the land in turmoil and paying little attention to the authority of the crown, the Jews as a well-to-do middle class played an important role. It was they for the most part who advanced to the kings the funds for their wars against the Moors. And when the Cortes of the cities voted the necessary taxes for this purpose, the kings gladly handed over to their skilled and capable Jewish "privados" the task of collecting these imposts.

They, in the meantime, carried on the wars with the sums that had been advanced them against this expected income. It was natural to expect, therefore, that the Jews would remain loyal to the crown, and the crown to them. The tragic fate of the unhappy King Pedro, unfairly dubbed "The Cruel" by history, is a gripping saga of this Jewish loyalty for which death held no terrors and that far transcended any personal or selfish considerations. That this earned them the hatred of the nobility, who in their blind self-interest did not understand the national policy of the kings and combatted it, is not difficult to understand. It is also easy to see how it was that the clergy reacted to the influence of the Jews with an equally violent hatred.

The catastrophe had to come, and come it did in the year 1391. The storm broke suddenly in Seville, and left in its wake four thousand slain and the community destroyed. From thence it raged through Castile, and then it rolled on through the land with an iron ruthlessness. Thousands of Jews took refuge in the bosom of the Church, and with this the history of the Marranos took on a new direction and impetus. So hard was the fall, so deep the terror, that the new Christians (*conversos*) were at first in a state of complete and utter confusion. Only gradually did they slip into that surreptitious, crypto-Judaism which is so characteristic of their history. The Church made good use of the occasion and followed up this wave of violence with what Dubnow has called a "Missionizing Terror," utilizing every conceivable means of enticement and terrorization. Jews were compelled to participate in and listen to religious disputations, under the most adverse conditions; baptized Jews were specially trained and then let loose against their own former brethren (Geronimo de Santa Fé, Paul of

Burgos). The Disputation of Tortosa (1413–14), which lasted for an entire year, was one of the milestones in this development.

In the meantime the Marranos began an upward climb. They were rewarded with royal appointments. In the full possession of all rights, there was no restraining the abler ones among them. They attained riches and honor, but for just that reason found it impossible to evade their fate as Jews. They formed a special class, and at that one in the higher strata, and it was not long before these newly baptized ones were hated with an even greater venom than had been directed against the unbaptized Jews. The bitter envy of the poor hidalgos dogged their footsteps, and soon the cry went up: "These are not real Christians. Their Christianity is just a sham. They are wolves in sheep's clothing. They are Marranos (i.e., swine). They cannot be trusted!" In the year 1480 the Church set up the first tribunal of the Inquisition against them, and from then on there was no retreat.

The entire course of events is however best understood by an event which, in the course of the inner development of the land, capped the structure of national unity. The marriage between Ferdinand of Aragon and Isabella of Castile (1474) brought this development to completion. This union rendered the North so strong that Granada, the last Moorish bulwark, knew full well that its fate trembled in the balance. The two hitherto separated aims, expulsion of the Moors and extirpation of the Jews, became fused into one. The Church with all its artifices could not cope with the problem of the Marranos. It carried its problem directly to the royal palace. There, by royal decree, that which had begun by street violence, disputation and ecclesiastical coercion was finished. The Catholic Ferdinand and the Chief Inquisitor Torquemada—a monk animated by a corrosive hatred—worked hand in hand. Denunciations were rampant, the prisons were filled, the burning pyres smoked, properties were confiscated and families decimated. In the meantime the war against the Moors continued. Granada fell in 1492, and the last Moors withdrew to North Africa. Soon thereafter the decree was promulgated that ordered the expulsion of the Jews. On the 9th day of Ab, in the year 1492, 400,000 Jews left the peninsula, leaving behind them all their possessions. Four years later their Portuguese brethren followed them, after their children had been snatched from them and forcibly baptized. A great chapter in Jewish history had come to its close, and with it the portals of the Middle Ages swung shut. For just when the Jews were bidding a heartbroken farewell to Spain, a Genoese sailor, Christopher Columbus—possibly of Marrano stock himself—was weighing anchor for his great voyage of discovery which opened the door to a new world, in fact to a new epoch. What the expulsion of the Jews meant to Spain can best be seen in the fact that, despite the discovery of America and the wealth that streamed from it to the land of Ferdinand and Isabella, Spain went into a decline. This happened despite the brilliant and superficially prosperous reign of Charles V (1519–1554), who could say that "the sun never set" upon his great Spanish-German-American Empire, and shows what the Jews meant to the economy of Spain. Some of its vital arteries were severed by their expulsion. And just as Spain declined, so too the lands that gave a haven to the refugees enjoyed great periods of expansion and prosperity. Naples, Genoa, Venice,

Salonika, Constantinople, the cities of the Mediterranean, Toulouse, Bordeaux, and Amsterdam received them and profited from their initiative and industry. Not more than half a century after the expulsion, Spanish glory could be seen to be a fast fading flower.

21

The Awakening World
and the Slumbering People

Not only was a new world discovered by Columbus.
The whole world, indeed, overnight became new. The
Crusades had already begun to widen the horizons of
men, even of the humblest. A totally new world outlook
was coming into being. Hand in hand with this went an
enormous growth in trade and commerce. The great
commercial cities of Venice, Bruges, Amsterdam and
Hamburg shot up. During that age of invention and discovery the spirit of science, of learning and of liberation, begun by Arab and Jew and furthered by the Hohenstaufen Frederick of Sicily, received a tremendous
impetus. Humanism came upon the scene with its new
concept of Man, which was formed from the revived
studies of the great masterpieces of Greco-Roman literature, and which for centuries thereafter gave form and
direction to Europe's culture. At the same time, and as
a consequence of this new-found freedom, some of the
old Church learning became clouded over with doubts,
and Church authority began to totter. The development
of the natural sciences went on apace. New experiments
followed new inventions, and new doubts followed new
experiments. The Church, mistress of the Latin world,
began to lose its authoritarian hold upon the minds of
men. Was not the printed Bible now accessible to every-
one? Could not everybody who was able to read look at

it and see for himself? And did he not read, did he not see, did he not begin to form his own opinions and his own most personal conclusions about the Word of God?

The great unified structure of the Church began to crack apart. It braced itself for defense. It sent John Huss to the stake in 1417 and for years incited the peoples of Europe against the intrepid Hussites. It would have burnt Luther at the stake too, but it was now too late. The Reformation had come to stay, and with the Reformation had come the spirit of a new age, with its ideas of religious freedom, but also with its doubts and individualism.

In all this development the Jews played a lively part. We must keep in mind that, despite ghetto and persecution, theirs was an existence not at all cut off from life and time. Eldad Hadani, the Jewish globe trotter of the ninth century who brought news from the distant coasts of East Africa, preceded Marco Polo by a good many centuries in widening European horizons. Had not Hasdai ibn Shaprut, as early as the tenth century, sent Jewish couriers to the King of the Khazars, via Hungary and Byzantium, as far as the Caspian Sea? And had not the Spanish Jew of the thirteenth century, Benjamin of Tudela, journeyed through the entire Orient, reaching, it is reported, as far as Tibet and China? The Jews were masters of many tongues. They dwelt in almost every land and had commercial contacts everywhere. Their travelings, both voluntary and compulsory, had given them a cosmopolitan worldwide outlook that most other people had not yet attained. We have already described how they, along with the Arabs, nurtured the sciences as physicians and astronomers, making significant contributions to them. They guarded the cultural treasures of antiquity. They translated and interpreted Plato and

Aristotle, and all at a time when the European nations were paralyzed by constant wars and their kings and emperors were constantly beclouded with political fantasies. To Germany's princes it may have seemed contemptible when the Hohenstaufen Emperor, Frederick II, kept up his court and cultural contacts with Arab and Jew in the southern outpost of Europe, despite the ban of the Church. In reality, however, he was paving the way for the advent of Humanism and the Reformation.

But it was not for the Jews to enjoy the fruits that blossomed on the tree they had helped to plant. Europe's renascence and the awakening of men found them at the period of their greatest degradation and humiliation. The sufferings in Germany and the expulsion from Spain had broken their spirit. The frightful problem of the Marranos especially weighted down, tortured and confused the Jewish world. Whatever blossoming remained there was squelched by the year 1500. Such rays of light in the darkness as the emergence of Joselin of Rosheim as energetic advocate of the Jewish cause, the temporary growth of increased liberty in Toscana, Ferrara, and Rome, and the flourishing communities of Salonika and Constantinople producing men like Solomon Ashkenazi, the great Turkish diplomat, and Don Joseph Nassi, Duke of Naxos, must not blind us to the hard fact that in reality their social position was bad, and their cultural position reflected this. This was truest at first in Germany, but then it became true for almost all of the lands of Jewish sojourn. They were excluded from the merchants' guilds, deprived of their rights, forced into money-lending, exposed to countless taxes, tolls and imposts and squeezed dry by them. All that was left them was the occupations of peddler and huckster, of which they became the despised masters.

In view of these facts, it appears on the surface that the immediate occasion for the Reformation—the unlikeliest cause—was the struggle that raged around the Talmud. It was a struggle which the Christian Humanist and Hebraist John Reuchlin waged against the Dominicans of Cologne, who were spurred on by the renegade Jew, John Pfefferkorn. This battle grew into a great struggle between the Humanists and the "Obscure Men," and in a little while it went far beyond the Jews and Judaism to become the great tocsin of the human spirit that ushered in the Protestant Reformation. This bizarre contradiction is heightened by the fact that around this time (1510) forty Jews were burnt at the stake in Berlin on a false charge of profaning the host, and that Martin Luther himself, disgruntled over the failure of the Jews to join him, raked up all the medieval libels against them. And finally to cap it all, as it were, it was Pope Leo X—one of the greatest of the Popes— and not the leaders of the Reformation who not merely permitted but ordered the official publication of the Talmud, thus finally saving the book from its fate at the hands of the Inquisition. But the Judaism of the time was still reeling under the after-effects of the tempest of 1492. A spirit of dull despair and rumbling unrest prevailed. Though there were no great authoritative leaders, a wave of immeasurable longing and yearning welled up from the very depths of the tormented people.

To be sure, as we glance through the story of the Jews during the sixteenth, seventeenth, and eighteenth centuries, there are bright spots to be detected here and there. In Amsterdam a great and pulsating Spanish and Portuguese Jewish community had come into being. In Prague, a strong, autonomous communal life with its own city hall had been fashioned. In Poland the mass settlement of Jews had resulted in the creation of a sort of state within a state ruled by the powerful Council of the Four Lands. But the general condition of Jewish spiritual and intellectual life of the time was marked by a sense of expiation, yearning for salvation, and gropings after the secrets of the beginning and end of all time. What they saw in the world seemed to strengthen them in that point of view. The split in the Church with all its political consequences, the breakup of the Holy Roman Empire, the wars with the Turks—all these seemed to confirm it. While the stronger natures among them applied themselves with greater vigor to the study of the Talmud, not only their masses but also leading spirits from among the disappointed and downtrodden of the people lost themselves in the dark mazes of the Kabbala. They listened intently to the distant messianic calls, and were inclined to put their belief, without test or questioning, in the wildest fantasies. The profound book of the Zohar ("Splendor"), the source book of the Kabbala, had by the sixteeth century won a tremendous influence over men's minds. In its origins this book was much older than scholars are inclined to think, but it came into its own at the turn of the thirteenth century. That profound mystic, Issac Luria (1531–1571), became a renowned figure. Just when Pope Leo X was ordering the printing of the Talmud, the Jews of the world had apparently nothing better to do than to turn their attention to the tidings of the Ten Lost Tribes which the mysterious traveler David Reubeni brought them, and to follow with the greatest emotion the fate of Reubeni's young disciple, the Marrano from Lisbon, Solomon Molcho.

And so it went. When, about a hundred years later, the astute and brilliant Manasseh ben Israel journeyed to London to take up with Oliver Cromwell the question of readmitting the Jews to England (1656) he sought to strengthen his request by playing not only on the devotion of the Puritans to the Old Testament, but on the widespread belief in the imminent coming of the Messiah. The Christian world too was stirred by such messianic speculations. Germany, shaken to its very foundations by the bloody Thirty Years War (1618–1648), gave ear to the teachings of the Millennium and the awaited return of the living Christ. Thus the currents of Christian and Jewish emotional longing began to intermingle. At the same time a horrible wave of persecution rocked the Jewish masses of Poland. The Cossacks under Chmelnitzki ripped through the 700,000 Jews of that land, and the slaughter lasted for ten years (1648–1658). Just about that time, in Smyrna, a Messianic aspirant, as fascinating as he was weak and vain, arrived upon the scene to play the leading role in a Messianic comedy which developed into a bitter, disillusioning, heartbreaking tragedy. But the real hero was not Sabbatai himself—his personal career, curious as it was, is hardly worth the pains of description. The real hero was the entire Jewish people which, in its longing for the Messiah, rallied round him.They began to answer his Messianic call—first the Levantine Jews, then the Jews of Italy and Germany—until its influences reached Hamburg and Amsterdam. The admonitions and bans of excommunication of the rabbis who saw through it were not enough to prevent many a Jew from selling all his possessions to get together enough ready cash to be able to journey to and join the "Messiah." True, the whole furor ended in a sudden and ludicrous fiasco, with the apostasy of Sabbatai, but the confusion raged on for many years afterward, and is to this day not completely extinguished.

The awakening was a terrible one. When the rabbis took hold of the reins once more, they found the people in a state of mute despair. The only means they could devise to cope with the problem was to set learning above all else, and to make the yoke of the Torah heavier than ever. In Poland especially, where the people were bleeding from a thousand wounds, they reared up a spiritual terrorism that did violence not only to the individual minds but also to the spirit itself. To the study of the Talmud was applied every manner of hairsplitting casuistry. Dialectics, known as "pilpul," became an end in itself. There arose an aristocracy of the learned filled with pride and hauteur which discovered how to make itself useful to the moneyed aristocracy. In their tenderest years, children's minds were turned to this dialectic which had a somber sort of asceticism as its basis.

But at the beginning of the eighteenth century, a reaction set in, in Poland. Too long had the mind been nurtured at the expense of imagination. Now the imagination broke its bounds, but this time it appeared not as a Messianic madness, but in the form of a natural, vital movement—Chassidism. Upon the foundations of a sensitive pantheism, its creator, Israel of Mjedzybosz (1698–1758), fashioned his new interpretation of Judaism. Since God was indwelling in all things, there was a constant interaction between earthly and heavenly spheres, and therefore God could be influenced by the power of prayer. But this power demands the highest degree of optimism. Away with sorrow and fasting! "Worship God with joy!" (Psalm 102). Simple goodness stands higher than austere study. Even the unlettered

Am ha'aretz can be a *Zaddik,* a righteous man. Thus it was that Israel of Mjedzybosz, more commonly known as the Baal Shem Tov (the Good Master of the Name [of God]) replaced the aristocracy of the learned with the aristocracy of those whose power resided in prayer, the "wonder rabbis" or Zaddikim. He created that movement which we can consider the only and late blossom of those otherwise somber two centuries following the expulsion of the Jews from Spain.

The cycle of the mystic, Kabbalistic experience, which was a motivating force for the covenant people through those two centuries, culminated with the Chassidic movement. These were centuries during which the European world was going through such monumental changes, overthrowing its older authorities, founding its sciences and creating its new technologies. The times were bursting with new developments—the printing press, the mariner's compass, the development of the universities, invention and discovery. At the same time the power of the absolute monarchy grew—Louis XIV in France, Tsar Peter the Great in Russia—grasping for itself the shining fruits of these new advances while the masses of the peoples, without rights, enslaved and oppressed, lay helpless at their feet.

These are the only two centuries in all Israel's history in which world history not only did not pass through the Jewish people but completely passed them by, leaving them slumbering behind ghetto walls. But to say that it was a period bereft of all creativity would not be true. Ḥassidism is ample proof of that. Inactive? On the contrary. In the organizing genius of Joseph Caro (1488–1575) was found a man able to gather together and to compress all the halachic activity of the preceding centuries into the concise compedium known as the

Shulḥan Arukh (The Prepared Table). After some struggle it came to be recognized as the authoritative code of Jewish Law and Custom and took its place alongside the Talmud. Even though the Shulhan Arukh was only meant to be a practical handbook, and even though important contemporaries like Solomon Luria seemed justified in condemning and opposing both the book itself and the undertaking, nevertheless the manner in which the book took hold among the Jewish masses vindicated the accuracy of the compiler's intuition. In time of great distress there is the tendency to gather together a national heritage for its protection. And people in great distress look not so much for new creativity as for props of support that are ready and prepared. The Shulḥan Arukh, which was only a shortened handbook of a more extensive work of Caro's, became the strong support of Judaism in the sixteenth century and remained, rightly, just that.

We are still suffering from the tragedy of those two centuries. For, as the awakening of the peoples through the French Revolution followed the awakening of the human spirit in those days, the new age found in the Jews a backward and humbled people that tried to make up the three centuries of human progress in a few powerful jumps.

22

The Ghetto Splits Asunder

While Judaism during those two centuries wallowed in penitential asceticism and dark apocalypticism on the one hand, and halachic stagnation on the other, forces were at work from without, quite unnoticed, under whose impact the ghetto walls began to crumble from the outside. The new spirit could not be resisted indefinitely. Just as invention and discovery widened man's perspectives and turned them in the direction of new possibilities, just as Humanism awakened the human spirit and the Reformation resulted in its religious changes, so too the sum total of men's advancing experiences were incorporated in a new world system and definitive new world outlook. Nicholas Copernicus (1473–1543), starting from the idea of relativity of phenomena, developed the astronomical system based on the then revolutionary concept that the earth moves around the sun. That which in his thinking was only an astronomical hypothesis was thought through by that great Italian philosopher Giordano Bruno. By applying the idea of infinity to the Copernican hypothesis, he raised it to a system of its own with all its philosophical and ethical consequences. Bruno was denounced to the Inquisition for his bold thinking, and was burnt at the stake on the 17th of February, 1600. Galileo, carrying on the work of Copernicus through careful experimentation, was the founder of a new science—rational mechanics—but under the pressure of the tortures of the Inquisition he recanted in the year 1633. But it was left to the Frenchman René Déscartes (1596–1650) to reconcile the new teaching with the Church's point of view. Thus he was able to incorporate it into the traditional teaching, and thereby to open the world to it. By his threefold division of all substance into body, spirit and God, he met the demands of the times, reassured the traditionalists and set these ideas fermenting in their midst. From his philosophy, however, it was inevitable that the French materialism of the eighteenth century would emerge. Ever wavering between dogma and skepticism, it led on through Voltaire, the enemy of the Church, who "would have had to invent God, if He did not exist," and through that social and pedagogical critic Rousseau, right to the French Revolution. But it was Baruch Spinoza (1632–1677), alone, who achieved a spiritual synthesis of the entire body of experience, something which the French thinkers did not succeed in doing, something they did not even consider, concerned as they were with maintaining peace with the ruling powers. Spinoza was not at all concerned with the ruling powers, for the power that ruled him—Judaism—was powerless, and the foreign power—the Church—had no influence over him. He was a Jew, and, what is more essential, he belonged to a Marrano family which had returned to Judaism.

The return of the Portuguese Marranos to Judaism, the growth of the great Marrano-Jewish center in Amsterdam, and the consolidation of the Spanish Jewish refugees in the commercial cities of the Mediterranean do not alter the fact that the Church of the fifteenth century through its missionizing terror in every form— disputation, forced conversion, Inquisition—tore a ter-

rible breach in Judaism. The obliteration of the boundary line between Church and Synagogue, the open contacts between Old Christian and New Christian, the
secret bond between Marrano and Jew—all these were
important factors in imperiling the inner condition of
Judaism. On the other hand, the return of so many of
the Marranos succeeded in paralyzing the spirit of the
Church among them. What failed, however, was a successful defense against the new mechanistic world picture which stormed through the breach, and began
working within the Jewish spirit to weaken the firm
structure of centuries-long faith in God.

Philosophically speaking, Spinoza was in every way
a product of inner Jewish forces. He was schooled in
Jewish sources and began to carry on his work where
Maimonides had left off. His shattering denial of the
freedom of will marked him as a follower of the Spanish Jewish thinker, Chasdai Crescas (1330–1410), who
was the first to toy with this view. Even his pantheism—
like that of the later Hassidism—stemmed from Jewish
sources. It came from the firm Jewish concept of the
oneness of God, which helped him overcome Cartesian
dualism between nature and spirit. And he was influenced too, perhaps subconsciously, by the forces of Jewish mysticism as he wrote those famous words of the
intellectual love of God. Even though he rejected the
extremes of this mysticism as fantastic, he was nonetheless carried along on the current of its forces.

The rabbis, for whom fate prepared the bitter task
of excommunicating Spinoza, and of reading him out of
the ranks of the synagogue with austere ceremony on
June 27, 1656, are today commonly looked upon with
scorn. In spite of that, one must not treat their memory
too lightly. They understood the genius of the then only

twenty-four year old man before anyone else did, and we, therefore, must try to understand and respect their point of view. That they took this stand only after the most careful consideration, and proceeded cautiously step by step, indicates that they were actuated by feelings of the highest responsibility. Rabbi Saul Morteira and Rabbi Issac Aboab deserve that their names be remembered.

But for the rest of the world, Spinoza became the father of Enlightenment and the man who cut the bonds of all religion and tradition. For Judaism he represented another opponent of the revealed Law of God—a second Paul, though he himself never became a Christian. Since his was a pure and simple life, unhampered by emotion and fully consistent with his teachings, his teachings as well as his personality could have a greater effect than those of others. This influence became apparent only a century after his death, as the passage of time ripened his work. Since he used the God-idea, he confused many minds even among the Jews with his philosophy which had its sources in Judaism, and had reference to Judaism, but which was nevertheless the opposite of Judaism and of all religion.

A century later there lived in Berlin a Jew whose life was as pure, calm and unaffected as Spinoza's but whose philosophy, in contrast to his, lacked all originality. He knew how to present and interpret lucidly the thought of others—Leibniz, Wolff and the English philosophers—in graceful and effective contemporary manner. This man was Moses Mendelssohn (1729–1786). His thought dealt with the realms of reason, common sense, and the problem of happiness, and since, in his case, too, his life was an expression of his teaching, his contemporaries loved and admired him all the more as he

remained loyal to the laws of his fathers and lived as a
pious Jew. His life was intended as a model for his Jewish brethren. It taught devotion to religious ideals at
home and devotion to freedom of thought before the
world. He spoke and wrote a perfect German, and not
the least of his contemporaries confessed that few could
match him in purity and lucidity of style. In this flawless
style he set forth his philosophical views (Phaedon, or
Concerning the Immortality of the Soul; Jerusalem, or
Concerning Religious Power and Judaism) and translated the Pentateuch and the Psalms into German for his
fellow Jews. This Biblical translation was an announcement of policy and was meant to be a model. As a new
and unique appearance in the Jewish world it was
indeed a model. As an announcement of policy it was
even revolutionary. What the French Revolution
was later to achieve socially and politically in battering
down the ghetto walls, Mendelssohn's translation
achieved in the cultural and literary field. But Mendelssohn died just as the American War for Independence
was hoisting the banner of human rights, and just when
that banner was being unfurled in France. He did not
live to see how the peoples of Europe, drawing their
political and social conclusions from the new world picture, began the overthrow of feudalism and absolute
monarchy. Nor did he live to see the cult of Reason proclaimed the state religion in Paris. He was also spared
the pain of seeing how his own children had failed him.
He never would have recovered from the blow of such
an experience, particularly since, by his own admission,
he "had no understanding of history." Mendelssohn had
a horror of Spinoza. Lacking that sense of history, he
only had an intense premonition of the consequences of
Spinoza's doctrines. He did not realize that with his own

deistic philosophy of "Enlightenment" he too was an unconscious precursor of those consequences. His own daughters were converted to Christianity, and his son Abraham had his children baptized. Fifty years later, in the literary salons of the Berlin Jews, this mad flight from Judaism played itself out as a macabre jest and tragedy.

23

The Struggle for Equality

The development of the emancipation of the Jews was not to be checked. John Reuchlin was its prophet. Moses Mendelssohn wrested it for himself on the intellectual plane. And in the terms of the Edict of Toleration (1781–82) issued by the noble Austrian Emperor Joseph II, it received its preliminary formulations in European state law. With the outbreak of the French Revolution, it attained its complete fulfillment at one stroke. Emancipation, however, did not come easily or without a struggle. It was a result of a hard and bitter fight, and it was not until the last days of the National Assembly on September 21, 1791 that the Jews were granted the full rights of citizenship. Men like Abbé Gregoire, Mirabeau and others championed the final undoing of the cruel wrong of centuries of oppression. Its fulfillment emerged only because it followed logically from the teachings of the Revolution, based as they were on the ideals of Liberty, Equality and Fraternity.

In spite of this, reaction began to set in with the rise to power of Napoleon I. Napoleon did not really have much faith in the emancipation of the Jews. This is clearly enough indicated by the "Assembly of Jewish Notables" which he convened in 1806 and the series of questions he directed at them. Their whole basis pointed at the direction of the complete assimilation and disappearance of the Jews. The "Great Sanhedrin" which he later established was in accordance with his conception of having the same complete authority over Jewish affairs as its famous historic namesake had possessed. Naturally it did not have this authority and became nothing but the basis for the later charter of French Jewry. But the burning ideals of the Rights of Man swept beyond the frontiers of France all over Europe in the wake of the French revolutionary and Napoleonic armies. Emancipation of the Jews marched on too. In 1808 it reached Baden, in 1812, Prussia. What Prussian statesmen of the caliber of Stein and Hardenberg established in their reforms was further sealed by the fervent participation of the Jews in the various Germanic states in the Wars of Liberation. But with the Congress of Vienna (1814–15) that closed these wars, a wave of reaction set in. The Jews saw their newly-won gains snatched from them almost overnight. A wave of bitter scorn and hatred hounded the but recently emancipated ones (1820–25). Then the young Jewish jurist, Gabriel Riesser, who could not attain the post of Privatdozent in Heidelberg because of his faith, made their cause his cause. For forty years he carried on the struggle for equal rights with dignity and with force. It was a battle of honor for the Jews. His contemporary, Leopold Zunz (1794–1886), founder of the *Wissenchaft des Judentums*, defined this not as a struggle for individual or isolated rights, but a struggle for *The Right*. Step by step the struggle went forward. The March Revolutions of 1848 tore a breach in the resistant breastworks of reaction, but it was not until 1869 that the newly formed North German Confederation abolished all disabilities directed at religious differences. In effect, however, this law did not afford the Jews the fullest emancipation. It was not until after the First World War, which was terminated by the Treaty of Versailles, that full equal rights seemed to have been attained. For the Jews of Russia the promises of equal rights became a reality with the collapse of the Tsarist regime in the March and October revolution of 1917, but in all other lands of Central and Eastern Europe it was Versailles that seemed to usher in a new and better age for the Jewish people.

The development in Germany, bridge between Western and Eastern Europe, was characteristic, not only in respect to its political approach, but also in its intellectual and moral consequences. Prussia carried through to completion what Napoleon began. Quite consciously and deliberately, the "Christian state" aimed at the destruction of Judaism through assimilation, baptism and intermarriage. There would be no equal rights without the sacrifice of Jewish traditions. Given equal rights on paper, but denied their complete enjoyment in effect, equality of rights became the motivating idea and ideal of German Jewry. It colored all their thinking, and was indeed the central subject of all their thought. Thus it was that the state once again reared a distinct type of Jew against which it was again to turn venomously a century later.

During the Middle Ages, by forcing the Jew into money-lending and kindred occupations, it was possible to humiliate and demoralize him externally. But his inner life, his inner spirit, built on the firm rock of unyielding loyalty to his ancestral heritage, could not be touched. Within the walls of the ghetto, within the confines of his own home, the Jew was king, proud son of an ancient people, unbroken and unbent as a human personality, and in his own family life loyal to his God and pure. It remained for the political wisdom and "enlightenment" of the nineteenth century to shake these inner bastions, and indeed to change his very religious being. Emancipation for him took the place of the messianic Kingdom of God. In the place of his eternal, unchangeable Law came the idea of adaptation to changing times. No less a personality than Leopold Zunz could proclaim this conception to his contemporaries. Out of this point of view developed also the reform of the religious worship, and it was this newly developed "Science of Judaism" that formed the intellectual armory that was the basis for these changes.

The great positive contribution of that epoch is the systematic, scholarly summing up of the rich reservoirs of Jewish history and literature at the hands of such masters as Zunz, Geiger, Holdheim *et al.* To be sure, through the Reform movement and the progressive ideas of the time there was introduced the idea of relativity in the realm of religion, that is, the eternally valid laws. On the other hand, their contributions, beyond all the considerations of practical necessity, acted as a creative inspiration in giving a new lease on life to the study of Judaism. It is sufficient to cite at this point, as a product of that development, the neo-Kantian Hermann Cohen. Their achievements worked out the contradictions and, aided by the rise of modern ideas, was considerably instrumental in the clarification of religious opinions.

In the meantime the state continued its work from the outside. It placed a premium upon baptism. It placed a premium, moreover, upon the baptism of children and forced the Jews to alter their centuries-old standard of values. But here we reach a point that cannot be completely explained by reference to external methods of state. This "trading in" of ancient moral standards, in the final analysis, emerged not from any external state policy but from the great spiritual and social revolution of the nineteenth century.

24

In Our Times

The Napoleonic Wars and the Congress of Vienna that ended them created a Europe supercharged with unrest. Dissatisfaction was rampant and stability was threatened by a political background with explosive implications. On the basis of this unrest, the grim reaction that followed reared itself. It did not affect the Jews only. Its persistent attempts to restore the "ancien regime" to its former glory and the revolutionary counter-strokes of 1830 and 1848 weakened and paralyzed the general political life of the time. Despite this, the first half of this century witnessed the greatest revolution that the world had ever experienced. The great changes that were wrought in the transformation of the world-view during and after the Renaissance were now followed by the Industrial Revolution. The Empire of Steam conquered the world, with the Empire of Electricity following closely. The railroad, the steamship, the telegraph, photography, the auto (its inventor, the Jew David Marcus), the dirigible, the radio (the discoverer of the radio waves, the half-Jew Heinrich Hertz), followed one another in close order. They conquered distances, encircled the globe and created a new internationalism. Nobody seemed to notice in the meantime that the machines were beginning to gain a terrifying mastery over men. New labor methods developed. Work was standardized through the division of labor. In a word, the Industrial Revolution had arrived, and with it a complete revolution of all social ideas.

The ancient cry for a new social order began to be heard once again. With the Bible in their hands, the German serfs called mightily for it in the great Peasant Revolt in 1524. In the eighteenth century, for the first time there began a systematic, scholarly, scientific approach to this problem. People began to study the origins and development of human society, to trace back and to question the origins of property, and to attempt to define the borderline between private and public property. But now, when the Industrial Revolution began to divide up the world into two groups—employers and employees—socialism was raised to a science and created the so-called school of "Historical Materialism" which attempted to trace all spiritual and intellectual developments back to original economic causes.

The Communist manifesto appeared in 1848, creating the Workers' Internationale. It has remained to this day the catechism of the world-proletariat of Socialism. Karl Marx, the great theoretician of this point of view, laid the foundations of these new principles in his famous work *Das Kapital*. This book became the Bible of Socialism, which soon took on, in many respects, the outer forms, and indeed even claims of a "world religion" in its spread through the world. This religion to be sure had no God. In fact it became the center of Atheism. But nonetheless it had its dogmas, its theology, and its apologetics. Yet in spite of this it was animated by a strong faith in the salvation that it could bring in the establishing of a better social order. It was this factor that gave it its strong influence among the dispossessed and oppressed in the capitalistic system. This "messianic" aspect, with its intransigency, had something in common with great religious movements of the past and helps to explain much of its propagandistic success.

As Marxian Socialism began to spread out from Germany, there was only one force that seemed to be able to stem it—the force of Nationalism. The origins of Nationalism go back to the Romantic Revival of the 1820's in Germany. During the struggle for hegemony, first in Germany (1866) and then in Western Europe (1870–71), it developed a science as complete as Socialism itself. The heterogeneous population and the struggle for unity in the yet disunited land made the German soil fertile for the development of such nationalistic ideals. Men like Treitschke and Lagarde laid the foundation of its ideology. First united with the capitalistic interests, it then developed into the strongest opponent of the Socialist point of view.

It is impossible to understand the history of the Jews during the last century without reference to this development. The struggle for Emancipation that was the principal concern of the Jew of Western Europe had distorted his historic vision. The state, which rewarded his defection from his historic faith with titles and official appointments, weakened his spiritual and moral bonds. He had abandoned the traditions of his ancestors and had modified and changed his religious observances. He doffed the yoke of the Torah and assumed in its place the cultural baggage of the people among whom he lived, and whose speech and fate he shared, in the fields of architecture, art, music and literature. He had nothing to offer to this except a spiritual heritage woven out of piety, tenderness and spiritual yearning. The mechanistic world trend had already done its work of disintegration in the ghetto since the time of Spinoza. And now, when the revolution of the mechanistic era was coupled with the impact of these new ideas, the resultant ideology found its aptest disciples in the Western European Jew. He had freed himself from the ties of his ancient traditions and stood ready to accept the new ideas openheartedly. The Middle Ages had cruelly forced him into money-lending and petty commerce. Now he found himself in step with the world about him. With the spread of the principle of freedom of thought and freedom of trade that emerged from the age of Enlightenment and the French Revolution, he was able to take an active part in the development of the new capitalistic system. At the same time, the social ideals contained in his scriptures still influenced him, and when the cry for a new social order went up, it also quite naturally struck a responsive chord in his ranks. In very truth, the Jew of Western Europe became an accurate mirror of all the conflicting ideas of the age. His emotional and spiritual attitudes became, as Heine said, "a potpourri-like composite of heterogeneous feelings." This was complicated by the fact that the German state policy which has been referred to sometimes succeeded in driving the basically conservative Jew into the arms of the political opposition. While all this was going on in the West the great masses of Jews in Eastern Europe, centered in Russia and Poland, lived on, for the most part in grinding poverty, but up until the end of the nineteenth century in complete, integral devotion to Judaism. But when the growing, crushing yoke of Tsarist repression began driving the people inexorably in the direction of revolution, in Eastern Europe, too, Jewish youth in large numbers were won over to the movement, and the process of dissolution set in there also.

Summonses came from all over the world, each of which could have been a call to awakening. The hostile, anti-Jewish reaction of the 1820's had scarcely begun to wane when in the year 1840 the hideous blood libel, in all its medieval horror, cropped up once again, this time in Damascus. The harsh policy of forced emancipation inflicted upon the Jews by Nicholas I (1825–55) was climaxed by the persecutions of 1880–81 that resulted in the establishment of the hated Pale of Settlement. The year 1903 was marked by the terrible pogroms of Kishinev and Homel. At the same time Rumania arbitrarily declared its quarter of a million Jews to be aliens. Then came the World War of 1914–1918. The Russian Revolution and White Counter Revolution drenched the soil of the Ukraine with Jewish blood. The Jewish reaction to all these forces was toward emigration. They left the lands of the highest pressure to fashion a new home in lands where the pressure was at its lowest. The stream of emigration was mainly directed to the New World, principally to the United States. Here there grew the vigorous pulsating Jewish community of almost five million, two million of whom live in and around the great world metropolis of New York City. This influx into the lands of new freedom—though it aroused some aversion—acted as a healthy catalyst upon the older Jewish settlers in these new centers.

25

America—A New Horizon

It was toward the West that the eyes of the oppressed were turned in hope at this crisis. America, in the brief space of less than a century and a half, had emerged from a colonial wilderness as the foremost world power. Through its Constitution, based upon liberty and equality, it had become a haven for the persecuted of all nations. And in the remarkable growth of the American republic the Jew played a vital part.

It was Marrano-Jewish wealth that, in part, financed the voyages of Columbus, and Jewish sailors were in the crews of his ships. It was chiefly Spanish and Portuguese Jews who, coming from Brazil and the West Indies, first beached their ships in 1654 upon the shores of New Netherland and founded their first congregations on the eastern rim of the continent. Out of the oldest of these congregations the still-existing Synagogue "She'arith Israel" developed in New York. In 1657 Jacob Barsimson and Asser Levy were the first among the newcomers to be admitted to citizenship. From that time on, the Jews of America, increasing in number through steady immigration, did not shrink from any sacrifice in order to help their new homeland in all her struggles. They fought and served with honor in the Revolutionary War (1775–1783), the War of 1812, and the bitter Civil War (1861–1865) between the States.

But not until the nineteenth century did American Jewry gain importance. Though German and Polish Jews had arrived by the beginning of the eighteenth century, the first large wave of immigration did not come until the middle of the nineteenth century, when the Revolution of 1848 and the reaction following it forced the rebellious to seek a new home in a freer country. Later, the economic collapse after the Franco-Prussian War of 1870–71 compelled a greater number to emigrate. Up to the present time, they still form a separate class, typically bourgeois, marked by wealth and retaining some of the influences of German culture. Even to this day some of them still hold the leadership in many of the charitable organizations of the country.

In 1881 the notorious May Laws of General Ignatiev were issued in Russia. They drove masses of Russian Jews into confinement within the towns and cities of the Pale of Settlement. Penned so terribly in their ghettos, they sought escape, and soon fled across the ocean to America. This mass migration was repeated in 1903–04, after the terrible pogroms of Kishinev and Homel, and a third wave followed in the wake of the World War when the Deniken bands decimated the Jews in the Ukraine.

Thus in a few decades America became the new center of Judaism. Almost half of its five million Jews, obedient to the gregarious instinct of masses, remained in New York, which in the meantime had become anew "Mother and City in Israel," with a great Jewish press, Jewish theaters, literature and culture, and finally, a strongly pulsating Jewish social life. The remaining two and one-half million were scattered over the vast continent. In many cities Jewish communities of a hundred thousand or more sprang up, and in their course of growth developed important organizations and institutions.

But these Eastern Jews were in contrast to the earlier German immigration; they were not bourgeois but proletarian, and it was they who in the end gave color and character to American Jewry. Caught originally in the industrial sweatshops they soon began to free themselves from exploitation. First they organized in small workers' groups for economic self-defense, but in 1888 these were amalgamated into one organization. The decisive years for them were the years of the great tailor-strikes—1910 and 1913—the result of which was the formation of the two greatest labor unions in the world: the International Ladies Garment Workers Union and the Amalgamated Clothing Workers Union. Today almost the whole Jewish working class of America, about half a million, is unionized.

Within the framework of such a development it was only natural that these Eastern Jews, who until then had known nothing but oppression, should inhale deeply the free air of the new country and adapt themselves rapidly to the American way which aimed socially at sensible and useful action, politically at peace and security for all citizens of whatever creed or race.

The result was that here, as in no other country, Jews met the government with an infinite trust and confidence and put all their hopes in the spirit of freedom and equality for which this government stood. Simultaneously, they did not see or did not want to see that America was not always able to live up to that spirit, and very often met the great Jewish immigration with visible reluctance, even with social exclusion. They met such lapses from the ideal with the easy equanimity which is typical of a land of many races and creeds. Yet from such a social order one quickly learned to measure all things in terms of material success. Thus one attained comfort, wealth and power, happy that the government, by whatever party it was led, remained liberal and tolerant.

Everywhere in the teeming life of the nation gifted Jews began to appear in high positions; state governors, judges, scientists, philanthropists, and writers bore Jewish names. To the august Supreme Court came, in order, Louis D. Brandeis, Benjamin Cardozo, and Felix Frankfurter; to the post of Secretary of the Treasury, Henry Morganthau, Jr.; and to lesser seats of the nation's council, many others. Not all of them were conscious and religious Jews, yet it was significant that within a high capitalistic economy and society they represented the Biblical spirit of justice and, by protecting the working classes, they helped to counteract the monopolistic tendencies within the country.

However, all this material gain resulted in some serious losses. As the ideal of material success spread among the Jews, the old traditions began to grow dim and the knowledge of the Hebrew language faded. The second and third generations, especially those outside the largest Jewish communities where the pressure of the group still dictated the way of life, began to place more emphasis upon physical satisfactions and to neglect more and more the emotional and spiritual values of Judaism. The feeling of group cohesion which still remained could not prevent the spread of intermarriage. Many thousands were able to live unrecognized among the general population and thus lost all connection with the Jewish community.

The rise of Reform Judaism in America can be attributed largely to Isaac M. Wise. He was born in Bohemia in 1819, arrived in the United States as a youth, and became a rabbi in Cincinnati in 1854. He was the first organizer of the movement, published its first papers, convoked its first Rabbinical Conference, and founded its different organizations: The Union of American Hebrew Congregations, 1871; The Hebrew Union College, 1875; and The Central Conference of American Rabbis, 1889. After Isaac M. Wise's death his successors departed still further from traditional forms and drove those who retained some traditional leanings into the arms of the rising Conservative Movement in which Solomon Schechter (1850–1915) played an important part. Schechter, born in Rumania, reared in Jewish traditions, professor of Oriental languages at Cambridge, discoverer of the famous Genizah fragments of the book of Jesus Sirach, brought an already famous name to America when, in 1902, he took over the spiritual leadership of the Jewish Theological Seminary in New York. When that Conservative seminary was founded in 1886, the Reform Movement had already been flourishing for three decades, an advantage which could be overcome spiritually but not materially. The Conservative Movement soon followed the example of the Reform: rabbinical conferences were called—the Rabbinical Assembly (1901)—institutions were created and, finally, the approximately two hundred congregations scattered throughout the land were organized as The United Synagogue (1913).

Last to avail themselves of the advantages of organization were the Orthodox groups. Although the Reform group was and is materially the strongest, reflecting more clearly the American way and spirit, the Orthodox group remained materially weak, making up for it with a vital energy and enhanced idealism. Its Rabbinical Seminary, the Rabbi Yitzchak Elchanan School in New York, was joined some years ago with the Yeshiva College and is an attempt to combine a complete rabbinical education with an equally complete college education. Not only does it provide congregations with rabbis, but also tries to give a not inconsiderable number of laymen rabbinic-Talmudical knowledge. It is aided by a second Orthodox Seminary, the Hebrew Theological College in Chicago (1901), and by the corresponding organizations of congregations and rabbis (The Union of Orthodox Congregations, 1898; The Union of Orthodox Rabbis, 1902). Dropsie College, specializing in Jewish and Oriental studies, and the Jewish Publication Society (1888), both in Philadelphia, add to the spiritual life of American Jewry.

The growth of organization in the three groups—Reform, Conservative, and Orthodox—and their divergent purposes and ideals are also reflected in the scope of Jewish education. In this field as well the Reform group was temporarily ahead and established the form which the Sunday School was to take. This institution, nothing but an imitation of the Christian Sunday School, is today the visible symbol of the uneasiness of American Jewry, even of Reform Jewry. Providing but two lessons on one day each week, the curriculum was and is necessarily restricted, thereby making the transmission of Hebrew knowledge almost impossible. But the Sunday School was soon so deeply rooted in American Jewish life that when the Conservative, Orthodox, and Zionists (the latest group) appeared on the scene with their Hebrew schools, they could strike root almost exclusively in the large Jewish centers. The Sunday School has de-Hebraized the youth and has not succeeded in keeping it to Judaism and its traditions which are mostly bound to the Hebrew language. Thus a paradoxical situation resulted. While Reform became less and less able to hold the more orthodox and Jewish conscious element, it benefited on the other hand by this meager institution of the Sunday School. Ignorant of Hebrew, little choice was left to the youth but to join the Reform Temple which stressed an English liturgy, unless they turned toward the growing Zionist movement. Coupled with that the desire for social prestige also played an important part in bringing recruits to the Reform camp. Hebrew education thus remained a problem. In an attempt to compensate for this lack and for the loss of religious values the Jewish Community Center was formed. It hoped to accomplish this by integrating the various interests of the youth, the secular as well as Jewish, the physical as well as spiritual, in one house. The Jewish Center owes its growth and flowering to the Jewish Welfare Board, which gathered for the first time in 1917 with the intention of giving recreational opportunities to Jewish soldiers and furnishing them with social outlets. After the war the plan grew into a strong social movement and evolved into community centers.

But even they were only part of a development which had resulted from the separation of State and Church in America. Scattered as they were, the Jews suffered more from that separation than any other group in the country. Attempts were made to overcome these difficulties by creating Community Councils and Federations which tried to bring together the different groups under the common roof of one organization in every large city, thereby trying to supersede the old European Kehillah system which had for centuries proved to be the stronghold of Jewish survival. These Community Councils and Federations, the development of which is still in its infancy, indicate that American Jewry is on its way to overcoming the threatening danger of sectarianism.

Summarizing the accomplishments of American Jewry within the framework of Jewish history as a whole, one must acknowledge that all the possibilities of this scarcely two hundred year old settlement lay in its inexhaustible power. This power expresses itself not only in the wealth and large number of congregations but also, and even more significantly, in the dynamic force which proceeded from personalities, groups and parties, and especially from the strong feeling of solidarity among the Jewish masses of America.

In 1906 the American Jewish Committee was formed with the object of preventing the infraction of the civil and religious rights of Jews in any part of the world. This was a self-appointed assembly of Jewish notables who, influential because of wealth and position, took over the leadership in Jewish affairs and held it for ten years. Splendor and greatness was given to this group as well as to the whole period by a man who, born in Syracuse in 1856, became one of the outstanding jurists in the field of constitutional law. For years he was the most popular and the most generally accepted leader of American Jewry: Louis Marshall. His personality represents the strength, will power, and fearlessness of the American Jews. His fight against the Jewish policy of the Russian government, which finally led to the canceling of the Russo-American trade treaty, and his energetic intercession for guaranteeing Jewish rights in the minority treaties with Poland and Rumania after the First World War will preserve his name in Jewish annals.

But in spite of such accomplishments opposition soon arose against the American Jewish Committee, which had assumed leadership without the sanction of the masses. A young rabbi, Dr. Stephen S. Wise, who later became the great tribune of the Jewish masses of New York, joined the battle and in a struggle of more than thirty years rose to be the leading personality in American Jewry. In 1922 he established the Jewish Institute of Religion, a school for the training of rabbis, and gave the impetus to the founding of the American Jewish Congress. This organization was democratically elected. Though it was materially weaker than the American Jewish Committee, because its support came from the masses, its spiritual and moral strength was far greater. Its influence was reinforced when, in 1940, the Jewish World Congress, which had also chosen Dr. Wise as its president, moved from Geneva to New York and joined the American Jewish Congress in the common cause of the representation of Jewish rights and interests throughout the world.

Violent as may have been the collision of the numerous forces within American Jewry, the struggles which resulted were nothing but proof of the warm-bloodedness and vitality of this youngest settlement of Israel. The importance of the American Jewish community was manifested not only in its political influence, but also and especially in the work of charity. Never in Jewish history was charity practiced with such munificence and on such an international scale. It was philanthropists like Judah Touro, the first Jewish settler in New Orleans, the banker Jacob Schiff who years later joined with his friends in saving hundreds of thousands of Jewish refugees from the Russian hell, and the successful Strauss brothers whose generosity bears witness to this fact.

Under the promotion of such men, the greatest charitable organizations Jewish history has even known were formed. The United Order B'nai B'rith, founded in 1843 as a Jewish lodge, developed into a great international organization with a social and cultural program which today, through its Anti-Defamation League, contributes also to the defense of the Jewish name. The Sheltering and Immigrant Aid Society, "Hias," founded in 1888, and the American Joint Distribution Committee, founded later during the early days of the First World War, have provided a vast program of Jewish overseas aid. In 1893 the National Council of Jewish Women was established, and its original educational program has now been broadened to include a large refugee service. Finally, the Women's Zionist Organization of America, "Hadassah" (1914), took form and gained rapidly in strength. Its work can only be fully appreciated when we direct our gaze back toward Europe and observe the inner tumult which meanwhile has shaken and transformed European Jewry and Judaism.

During the time that American Jewish charity had, under the impact of political storm and revolution, grown into a more and more glorious rescue work for a whole nation threatened with extermination, another movement had arisen in Europe, invaded America, and conquered the hearts and minds of the Jewish masses throughout the world: Zionism.

26

Zion's Challenge

Parallel with the rapid development of a new and vigorous Jewish community in America, a great new idea was gradually ripening in Europe. This idea began to shed an entirely new light upon the Jewish problem. It was the challenging conception of the reconstruction of the Jewish people in their ancient land—the new-old idea of a Jewish State.

For many years there had been inner stirrings of this idea, and before long it became a dominant force in many significant Jewish minds. It was all tied up with the problem of self-help, of self-regeneration and self-liberation. Thus it was that, as a belated consequence of the notorious Damascus Affair, the outstanding Franco-Jewish cabinet minister Adolphe Crémieux brought into being, in the year 1860, the Alliance Israélite Universelle. It was his specific intention to make of the Alliance a great international institution that would act as spokesman and representative of the Jewish people collectively, to meet their common problems as a body. Within the space of two decades, however, the Alliance had become almost exclusively an advance guard of French culture in the Middle East and lost the vision of its original goal. Subsequently it broke up, thus making way for other institutions of self-help in other Western European countries.

During this period organized anti-Semitism was becoming an increasingly menacing force in Germany. After some hesitation the German Jews grasped the idea of self-help and several strong organizations came into being. Among them was the Centralverein der Deutschen Juden (1895), which, however, only went part of the way in meeting the problem, concerning itself principally with protestation and anti-defamation.

Nevertheless, signs were not lacking to show that a prophetic view of Israel's destiny was not altogether dormant. The first penetrating and sensational flash came from the pen of the "Communist Rabbi" Moses Hess, erstwhile co-worker of Karl Marx and Friedrich Engels. There appeared in the year 1860 his challenging book, *Rome and Jerusalem*, which gave the first cogent and powerful expression of the case for the national rebirth of the Jewish people. His was the voice of a preacher crying unheard in the wilderness.

A little later, in Russia, the modest movement of the Lovers of Zion *(Chovevei Zion)* emerged. It was dedicated to the task of Jewish colonization in Palestine. It was in these circles that the word "Zionism" first came to be heard. Concentrating on colonization on a simple scale, they did not as yet recognize the signs of the times, and when the brilliant physician of Odessa, Dr. Leon Pinsker, arose to awaken them to the dazzling idea of a Jewish State with his remarkable "Auto-emancipation" (1882), he was greeted with violent opposition, especially from Achad Ha-am, the eminent Hebrew essayist and popular philosopher who wielded great influence in Chovevei Zion circles in his day.

At this juncture a man whose voice was to be a clarion call, shaking the foundations of the Jewish world, appeared on the scene. Earlier, in 1894, like a festering disease long hidden behind the healthy exterior of an apparently flourishing democracy, the Dreyfus Affair had broken upon France with all its ugly implications of reaction and anti-Semitism. This jolted the Viennese journalist, Theodor Herzl (1860–1904), to a full and crystal-clear recognition and analysis of the historical situation. Himself an assimilated Jew, with very tenuous contacts and connections with his people, Herzl achieved a view of magnificent simplicity and directness, with the unerring accuracy of a great genius. He brilliantly brought to a swift and clear consummation what the *Alliance*, the *Centralverein* and even the *Chovevei Zion* had failed clearly to perceive and to articulate. In his pamphlet, "The Jewish State," he called for the immediate establishment of a Jewish State as the principal solution to the Jewish problem (1896). The nation must regain its autonomy, he proclaimed, it must return to the soil. It must, in short, after long centuries of dispersion and wandering, be reconstituted in its ancient homeland.

Hardly a year later, in 1897, he summoned the first Zionist Congress in Basle, where the famous Basel Program was formulated, which called for the establishment of a "publicly recognized and legally secured home" for the Jewish people. Although this part of the program was Herzl's contribution, its general formulation was the work of Max Nordau, a famous writer of the time, a staunch friend of Herzl's and one of his earliest co-workers in the great new cause. Nordau became the spokesman for the new idea, and for more than a decade his powerful oratory dominated the sessions of the Zionist Congresses.

With the first Zionist Congress, this new movement, which for two decades had existed as an unrealized idea, received form. There had hitherto been no organized body to carry the idea effectively to the Jewish masses. In August 1897 the organization came into being, and it is a great tribute to the vision of its founder that he did not look upon it simply as a Jewish party. He viewed it, rather, as a great Jewish movement. And he viewed it, too, to quote one of his greatest utterances, as the "return to Judaism that must precede the return to a Jewish homeland."

In direct contrast to Mendelssohn and his contemporaries, he was able, gifted as he was with a profound sense of history and not without religious emotions, to elevate a temporal plan of Jewish self-help beyond the limitations of space and time, and to set it firmly into the framework of Israel's historic mission. It was by doing precisely this that he was able to impel the Jewish masses into action. To the "New-Land" Palestine, they would have paid little attention. For the "Old-New-Land" Palestine, they were ready for every sacrifice.

Herzl lived to see the people awaken to the idea, but he did not live to witness its giant steps toward realization. On July 4, 1904, at the age of forty-four, he died in Edlach. Faced with terrific opposition in his lifetime, toward the end fought even by some of his own followers, nonetheless he was granted at his death hour what the Jewish people had granted to no other man in a thousand years. No sooner had Herzl shut his eyes and breathed his last than it became clear that he had become a national hero, the very symbol of self-liberation and national rebirth.

Theodor Herzl died of a broken heart. It was the unhappy Uganda Affair—the offer of England to give her East African colony to the Jews for settlement—that touched off bitter conflict in Zionist ranks which finally led to his complete breakdown and premature death.

The mantle of Herzl's leadership fell upon the shoulders of David Wolfssohn. It was a sorry heritage upon which he entered, a shattered organization split into conflicting groups. History has not been too kind to Wolfssohn, yet his true stature and great contribution will one day be fully recognized. It was this Lithuanian lumber dealer, a self-made man of superior gifts whom Herzl himself had designated as his successor, who firmly took hold of the reins of office. During Herzl's lifetime he had been his only friend and closest co-worker. After his death, he succeeded where his beloved chief had failed. He steered the Zionist ship of state with an unerring hand through the shattering breakers of the Uganda crisis, and brought it forth intact. To have saved the organization at a time when its enemies had already begun to triumph represents a truly remarkable achievement. But broken by partisan conflicts, Wolfssohn, too, died prematurely in the first days of the war of 1914.

A kindlier star shone down upon the man who suc-ceeded him in leadership. To him goes the credit for the greatest diplomatic coup that the Zionist movement has ever achieved—the issuance of the Balfour Declaration, on November 2, 1917, in which the British government promised Palestine to the Jewish people as a national homeland. This man was Chaim Weizmann. Even dur-ing the lifetime of Herzl, Nordau and Wolfssohn, the "Big Three" of Zionism, Weizmann had gained recog-nition as one of the leaders of the Russian Zionists. When the World War came, and the fine contribution of the Jewish Legion led by Vladimir Jabotinski at Galli-poli began to win British sympathy for the Zionist cause,

Weizmann on his part gave added impetus to that sympathy by his outstanding scientific discoveries which he placed at the disposal of the British Government and which represented no small contribution to the British war effort. Thus was the soil prepared for the issuance of the Balfour Declaration, and despite the fact that the scope of that promise was later consistently restricted, it will endure and confirm Weizmann's historic merit.

The Balfour Declaration catapulted Zionism out of the realm of starry ideals into the more substantial climate of reality. The tremendous accomplishments, in a miraculously short time, of the Jewish people in Palestine under the impetus of Zionism, the phenomenal growth of Tel Aviv, Haifa and Jerusalem, and the heroic creative effort of the Halutzim (Pioneers) began to attract the incredulous admiration of all, even of the non-Jewish world. Step by step the Halutzim restored fertility and productiveness to a land long neglected. With sweat and toil, and even blood, they transformed rocky and barren hills and malarial valleys into blossoming gardens. The miracle of Hebrew reborn, the magnificent revival of a vital and throbbing Hebraic culture in its ancient setting, symbolized by men like Ahad Ha-am, the essayist, Eliezer ben Jehuda, the language-builder, and Chaim Nachman Bialik the poet, add an aura of glory to a great national epic. These cultural achievements, and their climax in the establishment of the Hebrew University and the Jewish National Library on Mount Scopus (officially dedicated by Lord Balfour on April 1, 1925) serve to underscore the immense reservoir of folk creativity which was unleashed by the Zionist movement.

Hard upon the heels of attainments such as these came the task of mobilizing the mass of the people behind this great effort. Many were the difficulties, problems and heartaches that made Weizmann's path as difficult as that of his predecessors. However, after the formation of the Palestine Foundation Fund (Keren Hayesod), he succeeded in forming the Jewish Agency which brought into the work of the movement many leading personalities of the non-Zionist world.

During the years of the First World War, the great leader of the American Zionists and close friend of President Wilson, Supreme Court Justice Louis Dembitz Brandeis, had succeeded in winning American support for the Balfour Declaration. Nevertheless, the internal conflicts that followed indicated clearly enough that the Jewish people as a whole had not risen sufficiently to take the fullest advantage of the historic hour. It took the infinitely more cataclysmic blows that came later to open the eyes of the Jewish masses, and to transform Palestine from the glorious reality which it had become, directly after the Balfour Declaration, to the terribly pressing necessity which it has become today.

We must not forget that Zionism, too, like all other Jewish movements of the past century, had to grapple with the dangerous threat of secularization. The disruptive spirit of the times had violently battered its way through the ramparts of the People of the Book. Jewish youth, to which the movement looked for such active support, had, in the East under the impact of Tsarist oppression, thrown much of its weight into the revolutionary movements that had arisen to combat it. In the West it had become assimilated and secularized. In the West as in the East, the mechanical and industrial revolution had done its work thoroughly. It tended to liquidate the ancient religious values, and it undermined the hallowed traditions of the people. These tendencies were even to be observed, in some measure, among the very youth who toiled in Palestine.

Even in Herzl's day, the throne of these older values had been usurped by the newer ideas of nationalism and Marxian Socialism, and were too well entrenched to give way easily to the idea of Jewish rejuvenation.

Meanwhile world history was marching on inexorably, with giant strides. In defeated Germany new and ferocious forces were coming to light. These forces which were nurtured upon the passions of hate and revenge of a vanquished people culminated in Nazism, and found in the earlier advent of Italian Fascism a willing partner. At first this movement appeared to be directed against Russian Bolshevism, but in the course of a very few years it became increasingly clear that the world was headed toward a shattering global war: the war of Hitler and his Nazi hordes and vassals against the Judeo-Christian spirit, the spirit of the Bible and humanity.

This much is certain: this war, which has engulfed the world in a terrible outburst of violence as these lines are written, is neither an imperialistic struggle nor a fight to the finish between Capitalism and Socialism. So far as Adolf Hitler is concerned, it matters not whether one empire falls and another rises over its ruins, nor whether a new social order emerges. For him this is primarily a war against Judah, nothing more. This may sound like an arrogant claim from the pen of a Jewish historian. And yet it is profoundly true, and is further testimony to the eternal survival of Israel, the great mystery of world history. Though a hundred times a perjurer and master in the making and breaking of treaties, on this one point, at least, Adolf Hitler has never contradicted himself, and ever proclaims it as his firmest and most inward conviction—that the Jew must be destroyed. And not only when he burns synagogues and murders Jews, but even when he persecutes the Church and imprisons priests—it is the eternal Jew that he has in mind. Not only when he razes ghettos and extermi-nates entire Jewish settlements, but even when he enslaves entire nations and tries to strangle their spirit—it is the eternal Jew that he has in mind. Nor does he mean the Jew who in the Eastern or Western hemisphere has carried on trade and commerce, nor the Jew who has widened the horizons of science and learn-ing by his outstanding inventions and discoveries. No, it is the People of God, the People of the Prophets and the Psalms, the People that proclaimed justice and righ-teousness, love and peace to the world. It is, in effect, basically speaking, God Himself that he has in mind, and Whom he would presume to drive from the very face of the earth if he but could. And in his eyes, in this respect, the Christian is nothing more nor less than a Jew in disguise.

History repeats itself. Once again, as in the days of Isaiah and Jeremiah, Israel finds itself between the upper and nether millstones of two empires. On the one hand is the Empire of Materialism, and its inevitable descendant, violence; and on the other hand is the Empire of the Divine Law, and its inevitable descen-dant, Humanity. The powers of the world are now engaged in a life and death struggle over this issue. All eyes are now on Palestine. It stands at the very cross-roads of time, and the Jewish masses throughout the world are waiting to see how the issues will be decided. On two scores the die has already been cast: the achieve-ments of Hebrew reborn and the Hebraizing of the Jew-ish world are accomplishments of incalculable consequences. Of even greater consequence is the visible reality of Jewish toil on Jewish soil. But toil of itself is not so much for something new as it is for the renewal of something old that is imperishable. There can be no salvation for this people, a people with such a history, at the expense of God. To secularize Judaism would be to liquidate its history. And no people surging with life and vitality liquidates its own history. There is still enough faithfulness and loyalty left in the Jewish world. It is faithfulness and loyalty that has trust in God acting through history, and in the inspirational atmosphere of the "Old-New-Land," which, in the words of an ancient proverb, "makes us wise!"

Epilogue

War and Holocaust

On September 1, 1939, Adolph Hitler's resurrected military machine swept into Poland. The world was engulfed by war and was never the same again. The bid for global power, a Thousand Year Reich and a world without Jews was unleashed. The rise to power was made possible, among other things, by ambivalence on the part of Britain, France and the United States, and the illusion that appeasement would satisfy the voracious appetite of the "wave of the future" on the one hand, and an opportunistic non-aggression pact with the Soviet Union on the other. It was encouraged, too, by lack of serious Western response to the use of anti-Semitism as national and international policy, with havens of refuge closed to millions of Jews seeking them, and the doors of what was then Palestine, a British mandate, slammed shut when it was needed most.

Austria had been incorporated into the Reich, Czechoslovakia dismantled, France, Holland, the Balkans and the Baltic States overrun and made vassal, and Western Europe turned into a huge springboard for attack on the British Isles to finalize control of the Continent. Japan, emboldened by this success, bombed Pearl Harbor, overran Southeast Asia and the Philippines, unleashing what seemed to be a global thrust for a New Order.

Prior to the invasion of Poland, hardly more than a hundred thousand German and Austrian Jews had managed to escape to the incipient Jewish homeland in Palestine, to the United States, Western Europe, Latin America and even Eastern Manchuria and Shanghai. The sun no longer set on the empire of Jewish dispersal. When the World Zionist Congress met in Switzerland in August of 1939, it hastily adjourned because war was breaking out. The sense of foreboding among the delegates as they departed, preparing to return to their respective homes, was weighed down with a deep feeling of impending doom. "Who knows if we shall ever meet again?" was the tone of the tear-stained farewells between Central and Eastern European Jews and their Western counterparts.

The Jews of Europe were trapped in the conquest, and quickly rounded up for deportation to the East, to Poland, to be plundered and used as forced labor for the German war machine, and finally eliminated in what was euphemistically termed a "final solution." By 1941, with almost all of Europe in Hitler's grasp, and the British Isles at bay, the Fuehrer unleashed his battalions against the Soviet Union, and three million more Jews were entrapped. The Nazis packed the Jews into ghettos, and then moved them to forced labor-extermination centers that were set up all over Poland. When the smoke settled, six million Jews, among them a million children, almost eighty percent of the Jewish population of Europe, almost one-third of the world Jewish population, had perished. This does not include the military casualties of the carnage, and the civilian casualties of the movement of armies and the rain of bombs from the air, and ultimate use of the atom bomb, all of which left casualties around the world in tens of millions.

But only the Jew as Jew had been sentenced to extermination simply because he was there. His very right to exist was put into question, a question which to this day has not been fully resolved in the minds of some. There was, indeed, despite the widespread carnage, something unique about the Holocaust. Only the Jews were targeted for death by the cold and conscious policy of the Nazi regime, whose anti-Semitism was wedded to cold, technical efficiency to target Jews for destruction simply because they were Jews. It is a regrettable fact, that in this the Nazis found encouragement in the fact that as they took their racist steps one at a time, resuscitating medieval hatreds with a diabolic slant by giving them a twentieth century veneer, in the West the reaction was a callous indifference that seemed to give tacit consent.

To be sure there were heroic gestures of help here and there: the Danes, a Raul Wallenberg, a Bultmann, a Roncalli, a Polish peasant and a German burgher here and there, but on close scrutiny the record is not one of which western civilization could be proud, not in the American State Department nor the British Foreign Office nor the Quai d'Orsai. To paraphrase a Canadian bureaucrat in the Department of External Affairs in response to efforts to save what Jews could be saved through immigration visas to Canada, "None is too many" is the reply history records.

Auschwitz, Treblinka, Sobibor, Bergen Belsen, Dachau and their like entered the human vocabulary as synonyms of unspeakable horror. At Babi Yar and Auschwitz one needed to struggle to remind the world that here Jews died as Jews, died, in the deepest sense, because, in the Judeo-Christian heritage they bequeathed to the world, they symbolized a quality of humanity and conscience which Nazism felt needed to be totally eliminated.

Auschwitz sits somberly behind a little forest and a town with neat, quiet homes, as though to symbolize how close together were quiet habitation and human horror, and how this terrifying reality must never be forgotten.

The State Is Born

It was a brief moment of grace. It was the kind of miracle that made you think of the parting of the Red Sea. The United States and the Soviet Union, allies in the War against Hitlerism, with conflicting interests almost everywhere in the world thereafter, saw eye to eye for a brief moment in history on the emergence of the State of Israel.

Their agreement made possible the political decision for the partition of Palestine in 1947, dividing the country between Arab and Jew. This decision by the United Nations, ratified by a two-to-one vote, set the stage for the emergence of the State of Israel, a possibility that it would have been difficult to imagine in subsequent years characterized by tension between the East and West blocs of nations. Behind this decision was a logic of history, pressed forward by overwhelming Jewish need emerging from the horror of the Holocaust.

Jews could not return to the graveyards of Poland and Central Europe. This pressure, plus the homeland a-building in the ancestral land, and havens of refuge beyond the crowded camps closed, combined with an inexorable historical destiny, moved the process forward to fulfillment.

The Jewish people, stateless for two thousand years, never forgetting the glory of the thousand years they dwelt in that land, gave it their name. They produced a religious and national culture that was seminal in its world force and influence, as from its matrix Christianity and Islam emerged upon that stage of history. They never forgot the land God promised to Abraham's seed, wherever they lived, wherever they wandered. Zion was the center of their memories, a focus of their dreams.

It was the substance of the Messianic movements of the Middle Ages, the center of profound concern, and by the late nineteenth century it entered European history as a nationalist, politico-cultural movement, reviving the Hebrew language and literature, continuing settlement in the land and winning international recognition with the Balfour Declaration in 1917.

So the state was born—better perhaps to say reborn—and it was not an easy birth. Hampered by the British who had turned away from the original intent of their promise, violently opposed by its Arab neighbors who rejected partition and denied the right of a national Jewish identity to exist in the region, Egypt, Syria, Jordan, Lebanon and Iran, invaded to land to nip the birth in the bud. In a superhuman effort Israel threw back the invaders and proclaimed an independent state in May of 1949 with boundaries slightly larger than the partition plan would have provided.

What would have become the Arab State had partition been accepted was occupied by Jordan and Egypt. Jerusalem, intended as an international enclave, was divided, Israel occupying the western zone and Jordan the eastern. The war was ended not by a peace treaty, but by a series of armistice agreements to be settled ultimately by negotiations that have yet to occur. The Arab States and the national organization of the Palestinian resistance movement opted for continued struggle by whatever means possible. They refused to recognize the State, attempted to isolate it, and continued attacking it by guerrilla terrorist attacks and economic and political boycott.

The Sinai War of 1956 was fought to stem terrorist attacks from across the Egyptian frontier. In 1967, encouraged by the Soviet Union, the Syrians and Egyptians unleashed a war designed to destroy the State, but it resulted in a stunning victory for Israel which reunited Jerusalem under Jewish rule, and put the Golan Heights, the West Bank, the Gaza Strip and the Sinai Peninsula under Israeli occupation. The Yom Kippur War of 1973 was another effort, and out of it came a realization on the part of Egypt that some other war needed to be found. Anwar Sadat journeyed to Jerusalem and the first stage in a settlement process of a piece of land for a piece of peace emerged. Israel returned the Sinai to Egypt and the first peace treaty between Israel and an Arab nation was signed at Camp David.

Forced out of Jordan in 1970 the organized resistance forces of the Palestinians made southern Lebanon their base. That little country, living in a delicate balance of Christian and Moslem, was torn apart by a decade of internecine strife and was turned into a base from which Israel was constantly attacked. This touched off the tragic Lebanese War, which destroyed the military power of the PLO in Lebanon but left a wide swath of painfully tragic circumstances for all concerned in its wake.

Against such a background of constant struggle, one would wonder what kind of a state could emerge from all this. The achievements against the background of such difficulties and obstacles border on the miraculous, a quality that emerges from every phase of Jewish history in its millennial progression through time. It is the tale of the rebirth of a people and a culture. Once created, the state asserted its historical significance by opening its gates to Jews from all over the world. They came from the camps of Europe, from the mellahs of Morocco, Algeria, Iraq and Libya, from India, Afghanistan, from Bokhara and Brooklyn—from almost a hundred different countries of dispersion. A Jewish base population of six hundred thousand became a nation of three million.

It became a state of explosive vitality. It combined the most advanced frontiers of scientific and technological advance with ancient values. In science, in agriculture, in imaginative social organization as expressed by the Kibbutz, in music, art and education, the achievements have been extraordinary. Its democratic structure, where the fullest expression is made possible in a sometimes chaotic and often raucus manner, has a unique quality that captures the imagination and sometimes jars the nerves.

And this, despite a persistent and ongoing opposition that would treat the nation as a pariah, define Zionism as racism and attempt to make Israel that term of opprobrium that the word Jew had come to be in the darkest Middle Ages. The hope that dialogue and understanding, an era of peace and cooperation, might come to the Middle East continues to beckon elusively, yet with a deep sense of longing.

In its long journey through history, unity and security have eluded Israel in every age and every era. In the Biblical period it was north against south; during the second commonwealth, Pharisee against Sadducee, Talmudist versus Karaite, Hassid versus Mitnagged. It is not different today. The tension between the right and left in politics, between Likud and Labor, the between religionist and secularist, between Sephardi and Ashkenazi is central in a divided land struggling to affirm its existence and identity. External pressures on the international scene, whether the Communist bloc or the Arab bloc, complicate its problems.

Yet it exists, with the destiny of the Jewish people in its own land in its own hands. Dialectic and struggle was always central in the Jewish historical process, and it continues to be. Fulfillment may solve old problems but it creates new ones. Perhaps the answer, if answer there be, is to be found in not solving problems, so much as surviving and living through them.

The Jewish-Christian Dialogue

Judaism and Christianity are better viewed as siblings rather than parent-child in relationship. Both were reactions to the messianic thrust and the destruction of the first Temple and State. Both saw their roots develop during the Second Commonwealth; both had their common origin in Pharisaic Judaism, the one following the course of long range messianism, the other of "instant" messianism.

What sharper conflict can there be than between siblings? What wars are more intense than civil wars?

Christianity, with its instant messianism, opted for the Greco-Roman world, won the support of most Jews of that region, to say nothing of the pagan, gentile world, and conquered Rome by the fourth century, making Rome and Byzantium its twin capitals.

The struggle for the inheritance, for the possession of the "mess of pottage" was intense, with the sibling victor always trying to keep down and repress the sibling vanquished. The image of the Jew as deicide and rejecter of Christ, as Cain bearing the mark of his sin through history until absolved through conversion, translated itself in policies of separation, ghettoization and pariah status. Anti-Semitism was a dismal offspring of this policy.

Jews were permitted to live in an area as long as they were useful and then expelled when no longer needed. Pogrom, persecution and peregrination was their lot, with occasional interludes of creativity and hope.

In Europe there were occasional moments of dialogue, with Friedrich Barbarossa in Sicily in the thirteenth century, the Spanish peninsula in preceding centuries; John Reuchlin and Pico della Mirandola in the Renaissance period; Gotthold Ephraim Lessing in Germany in the eighteenth century and George Eliot and Emil Zola in the nineteenth.

In early twentieth century America, friendships between a rabbi and minister here and there, with perhaps the best known example, the friendship and cooperation of Rabbi Stephen S. Wise and the Unitarian pastor Dr. John Haynes Holmes, marked the beginning of a new direction. Interfaith teams began to tour the country, a rabbi, minister and priest, putting people of all faiths in awe because they were on the platform together, but the dialogue on the whole was inclined to be superficial.

As in so many other areas, Hitlerism and the Holocaust marked a watershed. Sensitive and thoughtful Christians began to examine themselves in a new light. They saw that the Jew, marked for destruction by the Nazi, really included Jesus the Jew, with Christianity as a form of crypto-Judaism, to be ultimately destroyed because it too was corruptive of the true, pagan, Germanic spirit it had deified.

These thoughtful Christians began to realize that the Hellenization of Christianity, the victory of Paul over Peter, had moved it too far from its Jewish roots, to which it was deemed essential to return.

Vatican II was symptomatic of this. Pope John XXIII, as papal nuncio in Istanbul during the war, saw the catastrophe at close hand and understood. There was a monumental shift in collective attitude to the Jew and Judaism. The same process went on in the Protestant world. A new awareness of anti-Semitism and its Christian roots and of the pharisaic, Jewish roots of Christianity that needed to be recovered moved the process forward from a dialogue of the deaf to a process of genuinely listening to each other and hearing.

What has emerged has been a dialogue of consequence. At the academic-theological level, Jewish and Christian theologians talked with each other. They faced their painful differences with candor and a recognition that one side did not have to convert the other. They saw that what they possessed in common outweighed their differences. They saw that the problems of bigotry and nuclear holocaust called for common effort. They learned to confront their differences. They had no illusions of instant transformations, but they discovered that they could talk with each other and learn from each other.

A Samuel Sandmel could write *We Jews and Jesus* and a Eugene Borowitz could give us a *Jewish View of Christology* written with friendly candor, a good deal of understanding and sometimes cutting force. A Clemens Thoma could write a *Christian Theology of Judaism;* a Heiko Oberman and Franklin Sherman could confront the anti-Semitism of Martin Luther. Jurgen Moltmann and Pinchas Lapide could co-author a book confronting the basic differences between Judaism and Christianity at their fundamental theological level and come out with a mutual appreciation of the two covenants, both to be considered independently valid. The view that the Jewish rejection of Jesus was not a curse but a blessing, for it took the message of the Jewish view of God and ethics to the pagan world through Christianity, gained wider currency.

In the Christian world there is a wider tendency to view Judaism with a deeper sense of understanding. More and more this is apparent as these issues are the stuff of the training of clergy both in Christian and Jewish seminaries throughout the world, and in the proliferation of departments of Jewish studies in major seminaries in America and Europe. More and more they recognize the dictum of Franz Rosenzweig that Christianity and Judaism are opposite sides of the same coin, "eternally at odds, yet eternally needing each other."

There are still problems. Christians still find it difficult to understand that the qualities Christians see incarnate in the personhood of Christ express a role in Judaism assigned to the Jewish-people-as-a-whole as God's suffering servant, and hence the Jewish concern for its peoplehood and restoration in Zion. The theological implications of the restoration of the Jewish state need to be taken into account.

But never in the history of the two faiths has there been a more open and positive dialogue. The ecumenical dialogue grows. Jews and Christians communicate more openly and in a relaxed fashion at the theological, clergy and lay level. The understanding grows. The messianic goal of total understanding still lies in the distance. But the realization of the need for a better understanding of self through understanding the other, and the onward march of dialogue, beckons to the future with its promise.

The Diaspora

Before the Hitler era, European Jewry constituted sixty percent of the world Jewish population, while three-quarters of a million Jews inhabited the Arab lands from the Pillars of Hercules at Gibraltar, eastward along North Africa into the Middle East. The Jews of North America counted approximately one-third, and in Palestine the Jewish national home numbered half a million, a scant three percent.

The Holocaust virtually wiped out Polish, German, Greek, Austrian and Czechoslovakian Jewish communities and reduced the Jewish communities of the Soviet Union, Hungary and Rumania and of Western Europe except Great Britain by a third. By 1984 Jewish population had recovered from ten million to fourteen million, a painfully slow recovery for a period of forty years while world population, especially in underdeveloped countries and in the third world, was making a quantum leap forward. This slow recovery reflected assimilation, a rising rate of intermarriage and a decreasing birth rate.

Viewed in terms of demographics, the change in structure of the Jewish diaspora before and after the Holocaust and the emergence of the State of Israel is striking to behold. Where more than half of world Jewry lived in Central and Eastern Europe in 1939, in 1984 it was a mere eighteen percent, concentrated in the Soviet Union, Hungary and Rumania. More than half now lives in the Americas, with some six million in the United States; and the three and a quarter million Jews of Israel now represent almost a quarter of the total!

France is the only country in Europe that shows a dramatic increase in Jewish population, rising from a low of less than a quarter of a million after the German occupation and the sordid Vichy era to almost three quarters of a million. After the United States, the Soviet Union and Israel, the French Jewish community now stands fourth, while in 1939 it was tenth. This can be attributed to the fact that the shift of Jewish population from France's former North African colonies after the Arab-Israeli War was divided between Israel and France, since many of them were French speaking and, in the case of Algeria, had French citizenship.

During the period of the Second Commonwealth, from the fifth pre-Christian century to the rise of Islam, the largest and most influential center of the Jewish diaspora was Babylonia. In the tenth to the fifteenth centuries it was Spain. From the seventeenth to the nineteenth centuries it shifted to Poland. In our day it centers in the United States, its Jewry relating to world Jewry as America relates to the Free World, enormous in influence and impact.

American Jewry, with its growing acculturation, its economic strength and political influence, played a crucial role in support of the emerging State of Israel. It was not, however, a one-way relationship. From Israel, American Jewry, as did the rest of diaspora Jewry, derived the pride of rebirth and Jewish cultural and intellectual nourishment as it became a pulsating and dynamic center of Jewish life. Immigration from the United States to Israel was small, but the interconnection was not to be underestimated.

From the early twentieth century through World War II, American Jewry grew and matured, becoming an integral part of the American scene on one hand, and undergoing a Jewish cultural renaissance on the other. The growth of the synagogue in all denominations and their seminaries, the burgeoning of Jewish studies departments in the universities, the growth of its wide range of secular organizations, and the breakthrough into every phase of American life, artistic, cultural, political and professional, are perhaps best summed up by the symbol of Albert Einstein migrating to the United States and Saul Bellow and I. B. Singer winning the Nobel Prize. The price of freedom has been assimilation and a rising rate of intermarriage. The latter, however, has been balanced by the fact that probably as many non-Jewish spouses in a mixed marriage converted to Judaism as did Jewish spouses in similar marriages go in the other direction.

In the other major center of Jewish population, the Soviet Union, the picture was different. Although Jews fought as Russian citizens against the Nazis as heroically and desperately as any Russian, and although the Soviet Union voted in the United Nations to make possible the emergence of the State of Israel and helped supply Israel with arms through Czechoslovakia in its War for Independence, there was a drastic change in the 1950's, in the last years of the Stalin regime. A sharp shift to anti-Semitism by a paranoid, aging dictator brought on the Doctor plots repression and the murder of Jewish intellectuals and Jewish artists. Soviet Jews could not freely have links with Israel and world Jewry. Zionism was branded imperialist and racist. Jewish education was made impossible. Jews appeared sentenced to mass assimilation.

What happened, instead, was a quiet resistance, a rediscovery of Jewish identity of children of assimilated and of intermarried Jews, who were shocked by the rise of anti-Semitism, and who, at great personal risk, turned inward to affirm their Jewish identity. The odds against them are enormous, but the heroism of an incarcerated Scharansky speaks volumes for what Elie Wiesel described as "the Jews of silence."

Within the Iron Curtain there are vestiges of organized Jewish life in the forty-five thousand Jews who are left in Rumania. In Hungary's freer economy, the eighty thousand remaining Jews are a visible and functioning community, with a rabbinical seminary in place, that even sends rabbis to the Soviet Union and ritual slaughterers for kosher meat to Poland.

In various periods of Jewish history there was, on occasion, tension between homeland and diaspora, but the abiding truth seems to be that they were and are really the obverse sides of the same coin. Diaspora Jewry, certainly that portion in the Free World, plays its role creatively in the lands of their citizenship. But they are linked in destiny with the land of their origins, and their brothers rebuilding it, to march onward into history as a people of covenant and purpose.

Post-Holocaust Jewish Thought

If World War I jolted the high hopes for the perfectiblity of the human species, World War II and Hiroshima left it in shambles. The presumptions of philosophy and science began to be questioned. The thinking mind moved in the one extreme to the hopelessness of existentialist aloneness on the one hand, and for a need for a God that cared and had meaning, beyond transcendence, on the other. God was either dead or had to be discovered in a new reality beyond the "defining away" of earlier philosophical and theological systems.

The Jew had thrown himself with great hopes into the arms of humanism and the promise of emancipation. It was not, however, total immersion. There were some who had their doubts and expressed them. And among those who saw the promise of freedom there were signs of dissent.

It was in Central and Western Europe, where the giants of philosophy and theology held sway, that this was apparent. Martin Buber blazed new trails in the transcendent quest and went back to Hassidic roots to find the embers of a vanishing faith. Gershom Scholem, rejecting the optimistic view of Europe held by the advocates of emancipation, undertook the monumental task of plumbing the depths of the meaning of the mystical streams of Jewish experience and the Kabbalah, returning to Israel to do his work in 1926. Franz Rosenzweig stepped back from the brink of apostasy in a deeper study of the *mysterium tremendum* of Judaism. Zionist theorists, political and cultural, did their work. It was all grist for the mill of individual quest and the perception of the group.

One must recognize the fact that the secularist, humanist forces deeply affected the Jewish world. In a world that enlarged the areas where religion did not count, being a Jew was no longer a handicap. Jews pursued secularity and gave up religious practice to fit into society. It is against this background of humanism that a contemporary thinker like Eugene Borowitz describes a kind of return discernible in segments of seeking and searching Jews as they confronted the aftermath of the Holocaust. Some went back to the security of an Orthodoxy, in vibrant communities created by learned, pious, observant native Americans. And some among liberals moved beyond reliance on secular rationality and sought to live their personal freedom with tradition as their guide.

This devaluation of modernity moved many Jews to a deeper, more direct spirituality. They faced up to agnosticism which much of secular Jewish life assumed, and found it wanting. The trauma of the Holocaust experience, long in sinking in, is the benchmark.

There is, for example, Elie Wiesel, snatched as an adolescent from the warmth and security of the simple faith of his Hasidic surroundings into the hell of Auschwitz. He comes out of the trauma silent, at first, the autistic Jew incapable of speech. Moved by the warmth and sensitivity of his reception in France, the torrent of his witness begins to pour forth, perceptive and feeling. His is a strange dialectic—anger at the silence of God at this dreadful abyss that witnessed the death of humanity; at the same time a passionate urge to confront God, to speak to Him, to engage Him in dialogue, to call Him to account—and to tell the tale on behalf of his contemporaries who vanished in smoke up the chimneys of the crematoria.

There is, for example, the young theologian Richard Rubenstein, who could not accept God as the omnipotent author of the Auschwitz nightmare. This was driven home to him in his conversations on the Holocaust with German Evangelical leaders, where Dean Heinrich Gruber, an active anti-Nazi, nevertheless affirmed God's omnipotent rule even over the events of Auschwitz. "I could not possibly believe in such a God, nor could I believe in Israel as the chosen people of God after Auschwitz." For him there is a void where once God's presence was experienced but Judaism has now lost its power. If Bonhoffer saw that the problem was to speak of God in an age of no religion, he saw it in terms of speaking of religion in an age of not God. He had become a kind of Camus in clerical garb!

And there is Emil Fackenheim, who asks whether after Auschwitz the messianic faith is not already falsified, whether a Messiah who could come yet did not come at Auschwitz has become a religious impossibility. He sees the response in a great *nevertheless,* by the nature of the fact of the people's survival out of the ashes. It may not have found its full articulation in thought, but it exists in the actual life commitment of the people. By his very decision to be and to continue to be the survivor becomes the paradigm for the entire Jewish people. Fackenheim sums this up feelingly with these words: "[After Auschwitz] the religious Jew still submits to the Commanding Voice of Sinai, which bids him witness to the one true God. He is now joined, however, by the secular Jew, who by the act of remaining a Jew submits to the a commanding voice heard from Auschwitz, that bids him testify . . . that idolatry is real in the modern world." The decision to survive, to bring children into the world, to rebuild life in a reborn state and in communities throughout the world becomes a ringing affirmation from one side of the Covenant that clearly implies the other side.

To this writer it appears that this perception of the Jewish-people-as-a-whole as God's suffering servant, as the eternal witness to a transcendent possibility, is crucial. Gershom Scholem dared to restructure the view of Jewish history that was fixed in the firm mold of early nineteenth century European rationalism. He demonstrated the shaping force of the stormy undercurrent of mystical and messianic forces which parallelled the rational as the subconscious parallels the conscious. He could see a direct line of historical purpose behind this conflict of forces.

The Jewish death at Auschwitz and rebirth in Jerusalem might have made Hegel, who once affirmed that no nations appear more than once on the world historical scene, wonder whether at least one people is not appearing on the secular scene for a second time, with consequences yet unknown.

27

Retrospect and Finale

A long journey of almost four thousand years lies behind us. It is the journey of a people through every land and all time, and over many highways. It is the journey of a people that drew its inspiration from many sources and quaffed the water of many founts. This people was neither always nor equally loyal to its God. Even in its younger days, in the desert it showed itself to be a stiff-necked people. In its own land it oft paid tribute to strange gods, turning now to Baal, and now to Zeus. But as often as it went astray, so often did it find its way home again. Often enough was it like unto other peoples. It knew hate, it knew discord. Civil strife and partisan animosities twice ruined both people and land. And when it finally took to the long and winding byways of exile, the basic, rock-bottom Abrahamitic idea showed itself strong and durable enough to survive the rise and decline of world cultures—to outlast time itself. Why? Whence? Because in this people, a people which the religious world has called the People of God, and which with conscious humility and unbending duty so characterizes itself, one simple idea, despite all bypaths and detours, broke through to a clear and eternal expression: the faith in an unbreakable moral law for the world, eternal and unchangeable. This people has conquered time itself only through the loyalty by which it found its way to the Law of God as expressed in the Torah. Shattering trials had come to test them. Shattering trials are at hand. As long as Israel remains loyal to his God, he will surely be able to withstand whatever fate has to offer. For only that which is of God endures.